A TRAVEL GUIDE TO

California
Gold
Country

# Other books in the Travel Guide series:

# A TRAVEL GUIDE TO

# California Gold Country

Stuart A. Kallen

LUCENT
BOOKS®

THOMSON
━━━━★━━━━™
GALE

San Diego • Detroit • New York • San Francisco • Cleveland • New Haven, Conn. • Waterville, Maine • London • Munich

**THOMSON**
─────✳─────™
**GALE**

**LIBRARY OF CONGRESS CATALOGING-IN-PUBLICATION DATA**

Kallen, Stuart A., 1955–
    California gold country / by Stuart A. Kallen.
    p. cm. — (A travele guide to)
Summary: A visitor's guide to the weather, wildlife, transportation, food, sea routes, mining, and cities of California's gold country in the year 1851.
Includes bibliographical references (p. ) and index.
    ISBN 1-59018-144-1 (hardback : alk. paper)
    1. California—Gold discoveries—Juvenile literature. 2. California—Description and travel—Juvenile literature. 3. Frontier and pioneer life—California—Juvenile literature. 4. California—History, Local—Juvenile literature. [1. California—Gold discoveries. 2. California—Description and travel. 3. Frontier and pioneer life—California. 4. California—History—1846-1850.] I. Title. II. Series.
    F865.K15 2003
    917.9404'54—dc21

                                 2002013079

Printed in the United States of America

# Contents

Travel can be a unique way to learn about oneself and other cultures. The esteemed American writer and historian, John Hope Franklin, poetically expressed his conviction in the value of travel by urging, "We must go beyond textbooks, go out into the bypaths and untrodden depths of the wilderness and travel and explore and tell the world the glories of our journey." The message communicated by this eloquent entreaty is clear: The value of travel is to temper one's imagination about a place and its people with reality, and instead of thinking how things may be, to be able to experience them as they really are.

Franklin's voice is not alone in his summons for students to "travel and explore." He is joined by a stentorian chorus of thinkers that includes former president John F. Kennedy, who established the Peace Corps to facilitate cross-cultural understandings between Americans and citizens of other lands. Ideas about the benefits of travel do not spring only from contemporary times. The ancient Greek historian Herodotus journeyed to foreign lands for the purpose of immersing himself in unfamiliar cultural traditions. In this way, he believed, he might gain a first-hand understanding of people and ways of life in other places.

The joys, insights, and satisfaction that travelers derive from their journeys are not limited to cultural understanding. Travel has the added value of enhancing the traveler's inner self by expanding his or her range of experiences. Writer Paul Tournier concurs that, "The real meaning of travel, like that of a conversation by the fireside, is the discovery of oneself through contact with other people."

The Lucent Books Travel Guide series enlivens history by introducing a new and innovative style and format. Each volume in the series presents the history of a preeminent historical travel destination written in the casual style and format of a travel guide. Whether providing a tour of fifth-century B.C. Athens, Renaissance Florence, or Shakespeare's London, each book describes a city or area at its cultural peak and orients readers to only those places and activities that are known to have existed at that time.

A high level of authenticity is achieved in the Travel Guide series. Each book is written in the present tense and addresses the reader as a prospective foreign traveler. The sense of authenticity is further achieved, whenever possible, by the inclusion of descriptive quotations by contemporary writers who knew the place; information on fascinating historical sites; and travel tips meant to explain unusual cultural idiosyncrasies that give depth and texture to all great cultural centers. Even shopping details, such as where to buy an ermine, trimmed gown or a much-needed house slave, are included to inform readers of what items were sought after throughout history.

Looked at collectively, this series presents an appealing presentation of many of the cultural and social highlights of Western civilization. The collection also provides a framework for discussion about the larger historical currents that dominated not only each travel destination but countries and entire continents as well. Each book is customized by the author to bring to the fore the most important and most interesting characteristics that define each title. High standards of scholarship are assured in the series by the generous peppering of relevant quotes and extensive bibliographies. These tools provide readers a scholastic standard for their own research as well as a guide to direct them to other books, periodicals, and websites that will provide them greater breadth and detail.

# Join the Forty-Niners

Visitors arriving in California gold country this year, 1851, will find a region that has been greatly transformed in the few short years since gold was discovered on the American River near Sacramento in January 1848. In the three years since that momentous discovery, tens of thousands of people have arrived carrying with them tents, buckets, shovels, pickaxes, and gold pans. Since most began their quest in 1849, all miners in the region today are generally

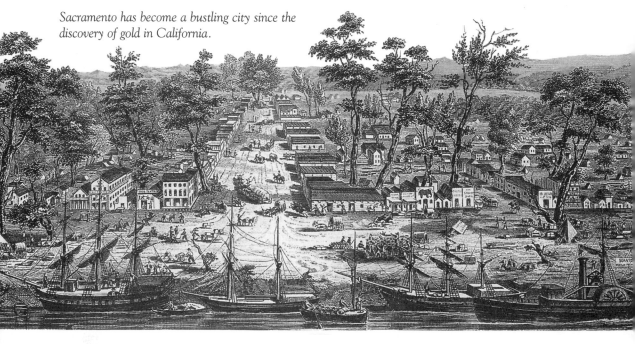

*Sacramento has become a bustling city since the discovery of gold in California.*

*A prospector's dreams can be realized in gold country.*

known as "forty-niners." Others refer to themselves as Argonauts, after the band of heroes in Greek mythology who sailed with Jason to find the Golden Fleece, the skin of a supernatural ram.

The forty-niners have arrived by ship, boat, horse, mule, oxen, and on foot from nearly every country in the world and every state of the Union. They speak English, Spanish, German, French, Italian, Chinese, and dozens of other languages. Some have been prepared to face the rigorous labors of gold mining by military service, agricultural work, railroad construction, or previous mining experience. Others are teachers, accountants, and businessmen whose hands are soft and whose arms barely have enough muscle to swing a pick and shake a gold pan twelve hours a day. But

the forty-niners all have one thing in common: the dream that they will become millionaires overnight from simply scraping the ground and picking up the fabled golden wealth lying within its rocky confines.

The goal of this book is to assist travelers who have the ways and means to travel to this exciting and dynamic part of the world. It matters not whether the traveler is a stout-hearted adventurer, a determined businessperson, or simply a tourist hoping to see history being made. This book will help those who need to know the best routes for travel and the best places to stay, eat, shop, and find entertainment. And travel tips warn of specific dangers or suggest ways to make the trip easier in the quest for gold and the fabled Golden Fleece.

# CHAPTER ONE

# A Brief History of California Gold Country

The long trip to gold country will give the traveler a great deal of time to study the land that lay at the end of the journey. But in the mad dash for gold, visitors often overlook the rich history of California, which dates back to prehistoric times.

The first residents of gold country, located in the western foothills of the Sierra Nevada, were Native Americans of the Yokut, Miwok, Nisenen, and other tribes. Fifty thousand Native Americans once lived here, but most have disappeared since the arrival of the forty-niners. Before the gold rush, these tribes occupied the region for nearly four thousand years, since at least 2000 B.C.

In their ancient wisdom, the natives had little use for gold. Instead, they practiced a system of barter, trading clothing, bows and arrows, food, and other items among themselves. They used no metal tools or weapons, did not have gunpow-

der, practiced little agriculture, and did not use the wheel.

Because of the warm climate of California, the natives did not require many worldly goods. The native men walked naked most of the year, while the women wore nothing but skirts made from animal skins or wild grasses. They lived in homes made from bark or reed matting attached to sapling frameworks. When traveling through the towering forests or wild river valleys, the Indians simply dug shelters into the ground, making temporary homes in the sloping hillsides.

Freed from the demands of the modern world, California's natives spent their days skillfully constructing items necessary for hunting, cooking, and storing food. Men made spears, clubs, and bows and arrows for hunting and war. Women artfully created baskets from dried vegetation, some so tightly woven that they could hold water and other liquids. These were gaily decorated with seashells, feathers, and dried flowers.

## Food Fit for a Gourmet

Though modern miners in gold country thrive on chicken, beef, and pork and beans, such American foodstuffs are not native to the region and were not essential for the natives' survival. The tribes instead lived on a diet of wild foods that

*Juan Rodríguez Cabrillo was one of the first Europeans to sail the California coast.*

would satisfy the appetite of the most distinguished gourmet.

Gold country natives ate fish from the rivers and shellfish from the ocean, and hunted a variety of game, including elk, deer, quail, and rabbits. The abundance of wild fruit and nuts in the area would make any forty-niner's mouth water. And while the acorns found on the abundant oak trees might seem exotic to the average Argonaut, this food was a staple for gold country natives. The bitter-tasting acorn seeds were dried, pounded into a flourlike meal, and cooked into a rich high-calorie porridge. In areas where there were no oaks, pine nuts or pods from the mesquite bush were served for breakfast, lunch, and dinner.

For thousands of years, California's Native Americans lived in peace. They were blessed with a great abundance of food and territory, experienced few wars, and had little need for kings, governments, or armies. Isolated from one another, the tribes spoke 135 different dialects classified into 20 different "language families."

## Europeans Explore Alta California

Unbeknownst to the tribes of the gold country, Juan Rodríguez Cabrillo, a Portuguese explorer employed by Spain, sailed into San Diego Bay in 1542. From there, he sailed north along the coast, mapping the shoreline and visiting Native Americans along the way. Cabrillo might have had contact with the tribes in the central region when he landed at Point Reyes near San Francisco.

By this time, the region had already been named by Spanish explorer Hernán Cortés, who first explored California in the 1520s. Although Cortés did not know of the riches found today in mining districts, he was the first to associate the state with gold. Thinking that the land was an island, Cortés named it California after a fictional tropical island laden with gold mentioned in the Spanish romance novel *The Adventures of Esplandián,* by Garci Rodríguez de Montalvo (published around 1510).

When explorers later learned that western Mexico was a finger of land attached to the mainland to the north, they called that area Baja California (meaning Lower California, now part of Mexico). The northern region, which they called Alta California (Upper California), included present-day California.

After this initial discovery, California remained unexplored by Europeans for many years. Then, in 1602, Sebastián Vizcaíno explored the coast of Alta California and claimed it for the king of Spain. The Spanish did little to protect their interest in California, however, until the 1760s, when Russian fur traders began to hunt for seals and sea otters in the area.

Spain wanted to prevent Russia from claiming the area, so the Spanish king sent Governor Gaspar de Portolá, Catholic missionary Father Junípero Serra, and a group of soldiers from Mexico to settle Alta California. They arrived in present-day San Diego in July 1769.

The Spanish set up a presidio, or military post, as well as a mission. The presidio was manned by soldiers and used as a trading post and supply house for military weapons. The mission was built to introduce Catholicism and European farming methods to the Native Americans in the region.

*Hernán Cortés, the first European explorer in California, named the region after a mythical island in a Spanish romance novel.*

## San Francisco's Mission Dolores

Travelers to San Francisco who are interested in historic missions will want to visit Mission Dolores on Sixteenth Street. This monument to religious faith, with its four-foot-thick adobe walls, is the oldest building in San Francisco and one of the six original missions founded by Father Junípero Serra. Construction of the mission began on June 29, 1776, only five days before America declared its independence from Britain. The work was performed by Ohlone Indians and overseen by Franciscan monks. The chapel was built six years later in 1782, and the ceiling was painted by Native American craftsmen with vegetable dyes. The brightly colored altar and statues originally came from Mexico in the early nineteenth century.

The Mission Dolores cemetery is also worth a visit. Mass graves contain the remains of more than five thousand Ohlone Indians, whose tribe was devastated by measles epidemics in 1814 and 1826. A large statue of Father Serra overlooks other gravesites of people from all over the world, including many recent arrivals who came here during the gold rush. Other notables in the cemetery include Father Francisco Palou, the designer of the mission and author of Father Serra's biography; Don Luis Antonio Arguell, the first Mexican governor of Alta California; and Don Francisco de Haro, the first mayor of San Francisco.

Between 1769 and 1782, the Spanish built three more missions and presidios in Santa Barbara, Monterey, and San Francisco. The presidios were surrounded by farm settlements known as pueblos, which were populated with mestizos, poor Mexicans of mixed Spanish and Indian descent. The mestizos worked the land in tandem with about twenty thousand Native American slaves. By 1804, a continuous chain of twenty-one missions stretched from San Diego to north of San Francisco Bay. Each mission was about a day's journey from the last along a coastal path called El Camino Real, or the Royal Road.

## Inroads into Gold Country

The Spanish proved powerless to prevent French, English, and other European explorers from utilizing the rich hunting and fishing grounds around the San Francisco area. In 1812, Russian fur traders built an outpost called Fort Ross on land about one hundred miles north of San Francisco. There, they trapped seals and sea otters and shipped their furs to China, trading for rich goods from the Orient.

Although the sea otters nearly disappeared due to intense hunting, there was still great wealth to be found in California. The climate is warm, the land is fertile, and oil, timber, and minerals are abundant. In

*Ivan Kuskoff founded Fort Ross as a post for Russian fur traders. It was later purchased by John Sutter.*

the early years of the nineteenth century, farmers, hunters, and traders from countries across the globe began to move into the area. Yet the countryside surrounding the rich deposits of gold remained largely unsettled.

In the 1820s, Spain began to lose control of its rich and distant empire as people in one area after another rose up in revolt. In 1821, Mexico gained its freedom from Spain and set up an independent republic. In 1822, the new Mexican government claimed all the land in Alta California. But the central Mexican government, far away in Mexico City, was torn by revolutionary conflict.

During the era of Mexican rule, which lasted into the 1840s, the Mexican government shipped political prisoners and convicts north to Alta California. The political activists started revolutions, and the convicts went on crime sprees. Neglected and ignored by the central government in Mexico City, local politicians began to compete for local power. But the biggest revolutionary change came when the mission system was brought to an end.

## Closing the Missions

In 1833, the Mexican congress ordered the missions to be closed and the mission lands to be divided among the Native Americans who were slaves there. Confusion and land grabbing followed this government order, and Spanish cattle ranchers seized most of the mission lands, leaving only the most barren tracts for the Native Americans.

By 1846, 8 million acres of mission land had been broken up into eight hundred huge, privately owned cattle ranches, called ranchos. Most of the land was taken by several hundred powerful men, including army veterans and friends and relatives of the Mexican governors. Mexican governors gave away the huge reserves held by the missions that included 370,000 cattle, 62,000 horses, and 320,000 sheep, hogs, and goats.

## Entertainment on the Ranchos

Enticed by the government giveaway, thousands of people from Mexico came to the area. Because most of the work was done by Native Americans, rancheros had plenty of free time to entertain guests and enjoy life. Social life on the ranchos was a lively round of feasts, festivals, weddings, christenings, wakes, cockfights, and horseback races. Church holidays such as All Saints Day also provided reason for celebration.

Parties sometimes lasted a week or more. Guests were served huge amounts of food and drink. Women dressed in bright velvets and men in embroidered jackets. They brought out violins, guitars, cymbals, and drums, and danced the night away.

The biggest, most exciting social gatherings happened twice a year during the rodeo. At this time, cattle were rounded up, counted, and branded. When the rodeo work was over for the day, it was time to feast. Cattle were killed and barbecued in pits dug into the earth. A large shelter was built from brush and reeds for dancing. The rodeo could last a week or more and included contests such as cattle roping and bronco riding. The rancheros bet on horse races and other games.

## Mountain Men and Ranchers

Most U.S. citizens who went to California before 1840 were explorers, fur trappers, and sailors. Some of the fur trappers traveled overland from the East Coast using the same primitive trails used by today's Argonauts. The first of these was Jedediah Strong Smith who, in 1827, walked across the Mojave Desert and over the Sierra Nevada mountain range with a ragged band of beaver trappers.

This group of hearty mountain men became the first Americans to explore gold country. They unknowingly stepped over rich veins of precious ore as they traipsed along the banks of the American and Sacramento Rivers. Smith found riches in beaver pelts, however, and one trapping expedition netted him and his two partners more than $54,000. The book he wrote about his travels, *The Southwest Expedition of Jedediah S. Smith: His Personal Account of the Journey to California, 1826–1827*, would make useful reading for any Argonaut on his way to California today.

# Visiting Sutter's Fort

Visitors to the Sacramento region can visit Sutter's Fort to see what life was like there before the gold rush. When approaching the fort, you will see the vast fields of wheat. Sutter also grows peas, cotton, beans, and barley, which is used to produce whiskey. The fields are still worked by local Native Americans, who exchange their labor for shirts, blankets, and other clothing. The crops are irrigated via canals connected to the American River, and young girls may be seen carrying buckets of this water to the gardens and livestock pens.

The walls of the fort, about 320 feet on each side, are constructed from adobe brick 2.5 feet thick and about 17 feet high. Although the property is now part of the United States, remnants of artillery once used to defend the fort from rogue militia remain in place. This fort was once capable of garrisoning up to a thousand men, but it is now populated by Native Americans and visiting miners. Inside the walls, visitors will find a three-story structure containing a bakery, blanket factory, blacksmith shop, barrel-making works, carpenter shop, and other workshops.

*Visitors to gold rush country can tour Sutter's Fort to experience what life was like when the area was a virtually unknown outpost.*

Many settlers followed in Smith's footsteps, including John Augustus Sutter, who was given a land grant of forty thousand acres by the Mexican government in 1840. In 1841, Sutter purchased Fort Ross from the Russians and changed the name to Sutter's Fort. Much to their chagrin today, neither the Mexican nor Russian government could imagine the mineral wealth that they were ceding to Sutter.

## The Bear Flag Republic

As the region began to fill with Americans like Sutter, President James K. Polk tried to buy California and other parts of the Southwest from Mexico, who refused the offer. On June 14, 1846, U.S. settlers captured the presidio at Sonoma, north of San Francisco. They proclaimed Alta California's freedom from Mexican rule and renamed the region the California Republic. The uprising was called the Bear Flag Revolt because the rebels raised a homemade flag with a picture of a grizzly bear, a star, a red stripe, and the words *California Republic* on it. The republic, however, lasted only twenty-three days. On July 7, 1846, Commodore John D. Sloat, the commander of the U.S. naval forces along the California coast, ordered the U.S. flag raised at Monterey and claimed California for the United States. After a short war with Mexico, the United States gained control of California. Official ownership was transferred on February 2, 1848, when both countries signed the Treaty of Guadalupe Hidalgo.

## There's Gold in Them Hills

That brings events up to the most recent years, and the reason so many people are traveling to California today. Just nine days before the Treaty of Guadalupe Hidalgo was signed, a carpenter named James Wilson Marshall, who was building a mill for Sutter, found gold. Although the nugget was about half the size of a pea, news of his discovery quickly reached San Francisco, and almost every man rushed out of the city to look for gold. Gold fever then swept through the towns along the coast. The pace picked up considerably in December 1848 when President Polk, in a speech before the U.S. Congress, declared,

> Recent discoveries render it probable that [California's gold] mines are more extensive and valuable than was anticipated. The accounts of the abundance of gold in that territory are of such an extraordinary character as would scarcely command belief were they not corroborated by the authentic reports of officers in the public service.[1]

Polk's words set off a stampede, and by fall, the news of the gold discovery had spread all over North and South America. Exaggerated stories began to appear in the press about people simply walking into the goldfields and filling their pockets with riches.

Since that time, travelers from across the globe have been heading for California.

Ships arrive daily from Mexico, South America, Hawaii, Europe, Australia, and China. In 1849 alone, about seventy-five thousand men came to the region, swelling the population to ninety thousand.

With so many people pouring in, California badly needed laws and a government. On June 3, 1849, the military governor, General Bennet Riley, called for a convention to draw up a constitution for California. The resulting constitution was modeled on that of Iowa, which had just become a state. It established the boundaries of California and declared it a state.

The convention elected state officials, a legislature, and two senators, who were sent to Washington. But even though California was acting as a state, only Congress has the authority to create a new state. So California's two senators, John C. Frémont and William M. Gwin, were not allowed to take their seats. After months of arguments, Congress finally allowed

*The discovery of a small gold nugget at Sutter's Mill transformed the history of California.*

*Miners gather to dig for gold.*

California to become a state. President Millard Fillmore signed the California statehood bill on September 9, 1850, making California the thirty-first state.

Today, the gold region has been completely transformed from a sleepy outpost of ranchos and missions to a bustling free-for-all of miners. Trails that were once used only by deer and antelope are now as busy as New York's Broadway, with bearded miners in dirty hats, flannel shirts, Levi pants, and heavy boots jostling one another on their way to the next big gold discovery.

# CHAPTER TWO

# Gold Country Location, Weather, and Wildlife

The region known as California gold country is located on a three-hundred-mile-long strip, about fifty miles wide, that runs north and south between the western slopes of the Sierra Nevada and the eastern banks of the Sacramento and San Joaquin Rivers.

In this large area of California's Central Valley northeast of San Francisco, gold is mostly mined from rivers that run into the Sacramento and San Joaquin River. The American River, which starts high in the Sierras, almost at Lake Tahoe, is where James Marshall first discovered gold in 1848. Since that time, the tributaries of the American, such as North and South Fork, and Weber Creek have been the site of much frenzied mining activity. North of that area, along the banks of the Bear, Yuba, and Feather Rivers—and their smaller tributaries—digging has commenced with great gusto. And those crowded out of the northern rivers might find their share of wealth south of the American in the Calaveras, Stanislaus, Tuolumne, Merced, or Mariposa Rivers.

Gold country is full of small mining towns that have sprouted out of the rocky soil virtually overnight. Some towns, such as Sacramento and Stockton, are developing into bustling centers of commerce where mining supplies are sold and assay offices weigh and buy the gold cut from the California hills. Miners, often bored and lonely from months in the diggings, fill the streets. They spend their painstakingly obtained money in saloons, gambling dens, and houses of prostitution.

Other gold country towns, many of them simply tent cities, are obviously temporary. These towns lack culture and civilized amenities but make up for it with colorful names such as Rough and Ready, Sucker Flat, Jackass Hill, Murderer's Bar, Red Dog, Gouge Eye, Timbuctoo, and Hangtown. Those who live there assume that the city fathers will find better names if the towns last longer than the small nuggets of gold within their midst.

## Weather in San Francisco

Sooner or later, all visitors to gold country will make their way to San Francisco. For those who have traveled overland from the East, the city by the bay will probably be your last stop. For those who have sailed around South America, San Francisco is the first stop.

Visitors arriving in the city will find a mild climate with pleasant, if somewhat cool, temperatures year-round. The nearby Pacific Ocean acts as a weather moderator, rarely permitting temperatures to rise above 70 degrees Fahrenheit or fall below 40 degrees. Regardless of the temperature, San Francisco is known for its fog—and for good reason.

In the summer months, mornings may be warm and sunny, but the heat pulls the

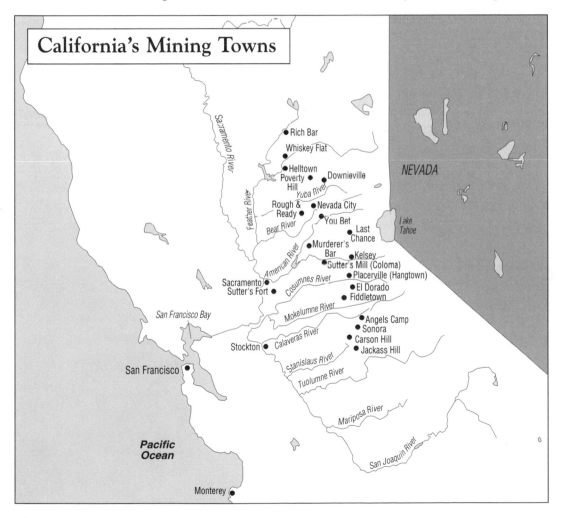

**California's Mining Towns**

Sacramento River

Feather River

Rich Bar

Whiskey Flat

Helltown

Poverty Hill

Downieville

Yuba River

Rough & Ready

Nevada City

Bear River

You Bet

Last Chance

NEVADA

Lake Tahoe

Murderer's Bar

American River

Kelsey

Sutter's Mill (Coloma)

Placerville (Hangtown)

Sacramento

Sutter's Fort

Cosumnes River

El Dorado

Fiddletown

San Francisco Bay

Mokelumne River

Angels Camp

Sonora

Stockton

Calaveras River

Carson Hill

Jackass Hill

Stanislaus River

Tuolumne River

San Francisco

Mariposa River

Pacific Ocean

San Joaquin River

Monterey

fog in from the ocean, and it rolls across the city like a wet, gray blanket. When this happens, visitors may be sweating in the hot sun one minute only to find their teeth chattering and their knees shaking moments later. Local residents know to pack a warm sweater no matter what the morning weather looks like, and tourists would do well to emulate this custom. In fact, locals joke that the coldest winters they ever spent were summers in San Francisco. As such, visitors from southern climes might find the city damp and chilly even in June.

The fog does not affect all parts of the city in the same manner, however. Large hills may block the ocean fog, leaving the eastern sides sunny and warm, although often windy. Meanwhile, large hills like Twin Peaks are exposed to the ocean and get the worst of the fog.

Visitors arriving between the wet seasons of November and May should bring rain gear. The city is mostly arid the rest of the year, but when rain does fall, it often comes down in violent downpours. Those standing near the bottom of San Francisco's steep hillsides would do well to move to higher ground.

Statistically, the coldest month in San Francisco is January, when daytime temperatures peak at an average of 56

*Taverns are a good place to catch up on conversation and recent mining claims.*

degrees and drop down to 46 degrees at night. Summers are cool, with the average temperature rising to only 65 degrees in June, July, and August. The warmest—and driest—season is fall, when 69 to 70 degrees is the norm, although the temperature may hit 80 degrees at unpredictable intervals. The best advice is to dress in layers, never leave your hotel without a sweater, and be prepared for anything short of snow.

## Weather in Sacramento and Gold Country

Sacramento, that great jumping-off point for gold country, has remarkably pleasant weather throughout most of the year. The climate is referred to as "Mediterranean," and is similar to that of Italy and southern France. This type of climate is characterized by mild winters and dry summers with low humidity. The winter months between December and February are usually marked by light rain and morning fog, with the average daily temperatures climbing to an agreeable 55 degrees. In July, daytime temperatures average about 76 degrees, with extremes reaching up to 93 degrees on the hottest days.

The average yearly precipitation is a little over seventeen inches, with almost no rain during the summer months. An average of four inches of rain falls in January, and it rains approximately fifty-eight days of the year. In general, the weather in Sacramento is warm and agreeable most of the year. The sky is often cloudless and blue, but the hot summer sun may send some visitors scurrying for the shade of a tall oak tree. Nights offer clear, starry skies, and when the moon is full, it is so bright that local residents claim that they can sit outdoors and read a book at midnight.

Although this might lead the traveler to believe that Sacramento is paradise on Earth, flooding in the city has been a problem. Even small rainstorms can cause the Sacramento and American Rivers to overflow their banks. The wide, flat plain where the city has been built is scarcely eighteen feet above sea level. As a result, major floods in Sacramento have created much misery for the citizens there in the few short years of its existence.

The main diggings in gold country are between nine hundred and seven thousand feet in elevation. As travelers climb various paths in the Sierra Nevada foothills, they can expect the sun to burn hotter in the day and the evenings to cool quickly after dusk. Daytime temperatures in August, for example, might reach 100 degrees and then drop down into the mid-50s at night. In January, snow-covered upper elevations may reach only 32 degrees in the afternoon, while plunging below 0 at night.

## Viewing Flora and Fauna

A wide variety of plants and animals can be found in gold country. Visitors will be pleased with the rich diversity of natural wonders in California.

In the southern parts of the region, golden rolling hills are dotted with thick,

# Flooding in Sacramento City

*The consequences of violent weather in gold country are harsh and dangerous, as the following article concerning the catastrophic flood in Sacramento City illustrates. It appeared in the January 4, 1850, edition of the* Golden Gazette.

This city has just gone through several days of dire disaster from the overflowing river. Several lives have been lost—how many is not known—and great damage done.

On the night of the 8th there was a great gale, accompanied by heavy rain. The next day the Sacramento River began to overflow. By the 10th the water had spread over a great part of the city. People and animals tried to reach higher ground.

Tents, sheds and buildings were swept away as the streets became rapid rivers, rising as high as the second stories of buildings. A new brick building at J and Third streets collapsed.

Hundreds of boats plied the streets, and they rented for as high as $30 an hour to frantic residents. Two men drowned in the streets when they fell out of boats. Many persons are homeless and completely destitute.

On an average the water rose six feet in the city, while the river was up 25 to 30 feet.

*Residents of Sacramento are caught in the midst of a dangerous flood.*

*A grizzly bear fishes for salmon. The bears are dangerous and unpredictable.*

gnarled ancient oaks and fragrant locust trees. In the north, the countryside is covered with cedar, pine, and redwood trees that soar skyward against a backdrop of magnificent cloud-scraping granite peaks. Between these immense hills and towering mountains are beautiful grassy valleys whose rivers teem with golden riches.

In spring, the hills above the turquoise-blue rivers are dotted with orange poppy, golden Scotch broom, and purple lupine flowers, while wild irises grow along the riverbanks. In the summer, a profusion of wild onions bloom in the fields. In the autumn, aspen, cottonwood, and other trees present a beautiful display of yellow, gold, and deep crimson leaves.

Needless to say, wild animals abound in these primeval lands. Grizzly bears are abundant, and visitors should be warned against tangling with these ferocious creatures. In the spring, the bears are hungry and ornery, and female bears with cubs will attack anyone foolish enough to approach. Unfortunately, bears are attracted to mining camps, where food and garbage are often recklessly strewn about. Travelers may avoid confrontations with the bears by storing foodstuffs in a duffel bag that can be hung from a tree branch with rope. Of

# Poison Oak Warning

California hills are beautiful to behold, but many trails and riverbanks are overgrown with poison oak, one of the most notorious plants in the West. While Easterners may be familiar with the burning and itching brought on by poison ivy, the poison ivy plant is avoidable to those who recognize the familiar three-part leaves on the small plants. Visitors new to California, however, are often unfamiliar with poison oak shrubs, which grow twelve to thirty inches high in the form of tree-climbing vines.

Poison oak is everywhere in California except in the hottest deserts and above four thousand feet. The triple leaflets of the plants are red, yellow, or dark green in spring and summer and turn bright red in the fall. Even after the leaves fall off in winter, however, the stems are still highly toxic. When the oily resin from this plant touches a person's skin, he or she can expect to experience a red, bumpy, itchy rash on the wrists, shins, neck, and face. After a few days, these miserable blisters ooze, harden, and then crack.

Travelers to gold country should ask local miners to identify poison oak in the field and go out of their way to avoid the plant. If the toxic weed is burned, those who inhale the smoke and soot may develop serious inflammation of the lungs. Don't ruin your trip by innocently stumbling across this cursed plant.

course, bears are often hunted, and their fatty meat is considered a delicacy by local Indians, as well as hungry miners. And stuffed grizzly bear carcasses are often seen modeled into menacing poses in local drugstores and taverns.

Wolves may also bother campers and have even been seen prowling through gold country villages. These furry scavengers will eat just about anything but pose little threat to humans.

The California mountain lion, which can grow up to eight feet long and 150 pounds, is another fierce predator found in gold country. Also known as a panther, cougar, or puma, this tawny-colored cat is one of the largest found in North America. Mountain lions live across California from sea level up to ten-thousand-foot elevations. They thrive in the hills of gold country, where their main food sources—deer, bighorn sheep, and elk—are abundant. Secretive and solitary by nature, the big cats are generally harmless to humans, unless threatened. Travelers who spot one of these majestic animals are warned not to make any sudden moves. Do not approach the animal, run away, crouch, or jump. Try to stand up straight and slowly raise your arms to appear larger. If the animal attacks, it may be repelled with a gun, rock, large stick, or coat thrown over its face.

Although gold country has its share of ferocious animals, visitors will see many more benign species as well, including antelope, black-tailed deer, coyotes, beavers, otters, and rabbits.

In general, visitors to California will find no shortage of awe-inspiring sights. From the near-perfect climate to the stunning scenery, this state would be worth a visit even if the gold in its rivers did not offer the dream of instant riches to lucky forty-niners.

# CHAPTER THREE

# The Overland Route to Gold Country

There are two ways to reach gold country from the southern and eastern regions of the United States: by foot or ship. This chapter is for travelers who intend to walk across the plains and mountains to reach California's gold mining regions.

Walking has several advantages. At two thousand miles, the walk from Independence, Missouri, to California is the shortest way to cross the country, about eleven thousand miles shorter than sailing from New York City to Cape Horn at the southern tip of South America. Walking also takes less time. By traveling ten to fifteen miles a day, a traveler can expect to reach California in about four months. Sailing, depending on the route and the weather, can take more than twice as long.

The overland route is also the least expensive, costing about $200 per person. By way of comparison, the sea route costs from $500 to $1,200 per person—more than a year's wages for most. And if a person already owns tools, wagons, oxen, and other necessities, the cost of the journey falls dramatically.

## What You Need to Know About the Oregon Trail

The most widely traveled route to the California goldfields is the Oregon, or Emigrant, Trail, which saw more than thirty-two thousand travelers in 1849 alone. The trail takes the tourist from Missouri through the territories of Nebraska, Wyoming, and Idaho and then connects with the California Trail in northern Nevada. The California Trail heads southwest directly to the goldfields of central California before ending in Sacramento.

These trails are river routes, blazed along the banks of several of America's greatest waterways. For the first third of its length, the Oregon Trail follows the wide and muddy Platte River, which meanders through Nebraska and Wyoming. The route then follows the Sweetwater, a tributary of the Platte, to the low and easy-to-cross South Pass of the Rocky Mountains. West of the mountains, the trail follows several minor streams before connecting to the cool, clear Snake River in Idaho country. After the Snake, travelers will switch to the California Trail and follow the Humboldt River down into the desert. After crossing this hot, barren land, the Carson River is a welcome sight, with its cool, clear mountain waters beckoning the traveler on to the goldfields.

Tourists on these trails will find sights of great splendor, such as rolling grassy plains, unusual rock formations, tall, snow-capped mountain peaks, and eerily beautiful deserts. These radiant works of nature, however, also pose life-threatening dangers. Hundreds of tourists have drowned while crossing rivers; others have died from drinking bad water or of thirst in the scorching deserts; and still others have perished in mountain snows. The purpose of this guidebook is to provide the cross-country traveler with enough information to make the trip a safe and successful one.

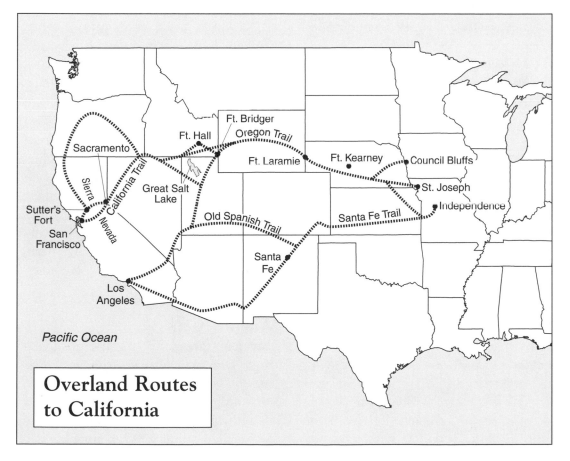

**Overland Routes to California**

## Take a Steamboat to the Trail

The Oregon Trail begins in Independence, Missouri, and is connected by three short trails to Council Bluffs, Iowa, and St. Joseph, Missouri. All three towns are located on the Missouri River and are known as "jumping-off" points for the Oregon Trail.

These jumping-off points are serviced by steamboats sailing from towns along the Ohio, Mississippi, and Missouri Rivers. Travelers will find no shortage of such steamboats, and prices to the jumping-off points are quite reasonable. For instance, passage from Peru, Indiana, to Independence is $5 for deck passage and $11 for a cabin.

There is plenty of entertainment aboard the steamboats. Itinerate musicians supply guitar, banjo, and fiddle music, and eating, drinking, gambling, and dancing are the rule of the day.

## Buying Food, Tools, and Other Provisions

Once travelers reach their jumping-off points, they will want to stock up on enough food and provisions to last for the entire four- to six-month journey across the country. The necessary provisions are widely available in the newly opened stores, where merchants are selling every imaginable tool and supply needed for the long trek.

The following food items will be necessary to feed four adults. The costs are approximate. Travelers will need 800 pounds of flour ($20); 200 pounds of hard bread or crackers ($10); 300 pounds of bacon ($15); 100 pounds of dried apples ($15); 100 pounds of sugar ($9); 40 pounds of coffee ($6); 50 pounds of rice ($3); and about 10 pounds of salt and pepper ($1.50).

Cooking utensils are also needed. Each wagon will need one tea kettle and coffeepot; two six-quart cooking kettles; one frying pan; a large can for milk; and four plates, tin cups, knives, and forks. These items weigh about twenty-five pounds and may be purchased together for $10.

Necessary tools include buckets, shovels, pickaxes, guns, ammunition, tents, blankets, India rubber ground cloths, and chains. Prices vary depending on where they are purchased.

*A note of warning:* Many travelers are tempted to purchase more than they need, fearing that they might require a particular item and it will be unavailable. It is advised, however, that travelers do not overload their wagons. Heavy items such as books and furniture quickly lose their value—sentimental or otherwise—when they need to be carted across rivers, through axle-deep mud, and over steep mountain passes.

## Wagon Facts

Travelers should choose their wagons carefully. After all, these vehicles will be carrying your family and worldly possessions and must provide protection and shelter from the elements under some of the harshest conditions imaginable.

The most commonly available wagon is known as the prairie schooner. These vehicles are about ten feet long, four feet wide, and two feet deep, and are constructed from hardwoods such as oak and maple. The seams between the floorboards are caulked with tar, so they will float across rivers when necessary.

Prairie schooners are so named because their white canvas coverings look like ship sails. These coverings are made from cloth that has been waterproofed with linseed oil and stretched across U-shaped frames inserted into the wagon bed. The wagon bed and covers are mounted on four large wheels with axles known as running gear. Make sure that your wagons are fitted with new wheels and iron rims; that the spokes are tight; and that the axles are greased.

## Choosing Pack Animals

In recent years, there has been great debate over which draft animals—horses, mules, or oxen—are best suited for the trek across the country. Some prefer horses for their speed and agility, but these animals are expensive—$40 to $50. In addition, since the animals cannot live on the grasses commonly found along the trail, the horses' diets must be supplemented with grain, which has to be hauled. Finally, horses require expensive saddles and harnesses, which often need repair or replacement.

Mules are also expensive and require costly leather and metal harnesses. For these reasons, it is recommended that

## Where to Begin

There are three major jumping-off towns, and dozens of smaller ones, along the Missouri River. The one that is best for you depends on where you live and where you want to go.

Independence, Missouri, is the most well-known jumping-off place, and in 1850, the town boasted a population of over two thousand. The streets are lined with wood-frame houses and prosperous businesses. Paddle steamers from St. Louis arrive hourly carrying hundreds of travelers from across the United States as well as from Great Britain, Germany, Russia, France, Italy, and elsewhere.

St. Joseph lies fifty-five miles northwest of Independence and has attracted visitors from the northern Midwest states such as Ohio, Illinois, Indiana, Michigan, and Iowa. Those who take paddle steamers to this little town can save a four-day walk from Independence, along with several river crossings.

Council Bluffs, or Kanesville, in Iowa country, takes the traveler north of the Oregon Trail, but seems to be the favored jumping-off place for visitors from the northern regions of Minnesota, Wisconsin, and the upper peninsula of Michigan.

*The journey West includes several river crossings. Here, emigrants make their way down the Snake River.*

travelers use oxen. These castrated bulls are docile, can live on the thin grasses found along the trail, and need only simple wooden yokes and metal chains for pulling wagons. Oxen are also cheap—$45 to $55 a pair. And two oxen are capable of pulling a fully loaded wagon that may weigh up to one ton.

Despite these animals' strength, the Oregon Trail is littered with the bones of dead oxen that have died from thirst, injury, and overwork. It is recommended that travelers bring at least two extra oxen, with yokes for each wagon, to replace those that may die in service.

In addition, don't forget to purchase a milk cow. These useful animals will provide a steady supply of milk and butter and will walk along happily while tied to the back of a wagon.

## Predicaments Along the Platte

With provisions gathered, wagons loaded, and animals well fed and strong, the journey begins. The Platte is bordered by sandy, grass-covered hills, and the valley of the mile-wide river is as level as a cabin floor. It is here that newly arrived travelers will join a seemingly endless parade of wagon trains with hundreds of travelers rolling west in a long, slow line. During this first leg of the trip, tourists will have little trouble finding their way as they follow the meandering muddy river for hundreds of miles through the Nebraska and Wyoming regions. As they travel along, they'll encounter boundless skies, spring flowers, and a variety of wildlife, including thousands of bison, antelope, wolves, deer, rabbits, and birds.

The placid Platte River, however, presents a unique set of dangers, for it is necessary to cross the river in dozens of places. This can be treacherous work: Steep muddy banks, swift currents, and frightened animals add danger to every step. Travelers should be warned that hundreds of people have lost all of their possessions (and some their lives) at the most dangerous fords across the river.

There are several ways to make river crossings easier. At shallow fords, wagon owners can loosen the bolts that hold the boxes (wagon beds) to the running gear and slip logs or boards in between to raise the bed about six inches. If this is not sufficient, travelers must unload all their possessions and lay boards or ropes across the top of the box. Since your box should be well caulked and waterproof, this should work fine. If the water is

## Travel Tips

*Here are a few travel tips to make your cross-country journey easier.*

- Sew pockets to the insides of the cloth wagon tops. These can be used to store everyday necessities such as soap, hairbrushes, cooking utensils, and small firearms.
- Get up early and get on the road by 4:00 a.m. Then stop to camp and sleep around noon, when the sun is hottest and temperatures are highest.
- Walk, don't ride: Wagons travel very slowly, and the bumpy trails make the wagon seats uncomfortable.
- Women might want to abandon their long dresses and wear pants.
- Making butter: After a few hours on the bumpy trail, a ball of butter will form in the center of a can of milk.
- Eggs can be stored in flour barrels. As long as they are not touching, they won't break.
- Hang a bucket of grease made from tar and animal fat between the wagon wheels to lubricate the axle.
- Wood is scarce along the trail. Pick up dried bison dung, or "chips," to burn in campfires.

flowing fast, however, this improvised platform might be top-heavy and capsize. In this case, it might be wise to construct a raft from willow branches and bison hides or bolt together several wagon boxes into a makeshift boat. If the currents are high and the river is flowing fast after a rainstorm and none of these options will do, travelers must camp along the shore and let nature take its course. After a dry day or two, the water will recede and crossing will be easier.

It may be difficult to stay dry during river crossings, but tourists along the Platte may find the weather even more vexing. In this region, there is little in the way of natural protection from weather, and you can expect torrential downpours, tornadoes, hail, thunder, and lightning. After such outbreaks, mud along the trail may nearly swallow wagons, and even horses, mules, and oxen.

## Stock Up at Fort Laramie

About five hundred miles into the journey, the prairie ends at the confluence of the North Platte and Laramie Rivers. It is near here, in 1834, that two mountain men built the fort now known as Laramie. Fort Laramie is made of adobe and enclosed by a high wall. This is an excellent place to stock up on provisions; the next outpost, Fort Bridger, is nearly four hundred miles to the west.

Inside the fort, travelers will find a scene resembling a small town, with men selling furs and food along with services such as blacksmithing and wagon repair. Goods are available, but prices are high.

*Fort Laramie is an essential refueling stop along the Oregon Trail.*

# Independence Rock

About sixty miles into the Sweetwater Valley, travelers will encounter one of the most famous landmarks along the trail, Independence Rock. This huge hill, 700 feet wide, 1,900 feet long, and 128 feet above the valley floor, was named in 1830 by William Sublette when he celebrated the Fourth of July—Independence Day—at the site.

Known as the halfway mark on the journey West, Independence Rock has been signed by hundreds of people since the 1820s, when the first "mountain men" in the area passed the site. People carve their names into the rock for simple reasons of pride. But it is also an excellent way for tourists to notify friends and family who are following behind that they have passed this way. For this reason, the rock is also known as the "Great Register of the Desert."

*Independence Rock is a well-known landmark and message center along the Oregon Trail.*

For example, flour is $18 per hundred pounds; whiskey is $8 per gallon.

About seventy-five thousand people passed by Fort Laramie in 1850. The fields surrounding the area are filled with campers who have stopped to rest, wash, and regroup after the hike up the Platte.

# Independence Rock and South Pass

About 150 miles past Fort Laramie, travelers will approach the valley of the Sweetwater River, where fresh, rapidly flowing waters and good pastures provide a stark contrast to the muddy Platte. Visitors should be advised, however, that the water in the many mineral hot springs and lakes around the Sweetwater is poisonous. Drinking this water can cause sickness or death. It is a good idea to keep guards posted at night to make sure that cattle do not wander into these alkali springs.

About five miles down the Sweetwater, you will come to the imposing landmark known as Independence Rock, which juts skyward on the north side of the river. The sheer walls of the rock have been inscribed by thousands of emigrants who, passing this way, have taken the time to carve or paint their names on its hard granite face. Those with the energy to climb 130 feet to the top will be rewarded with an awe-inspiring view of the snow-capped Rocky Mountains that lie ahead.

Past Independence Rock, the long, slow ascent across the high plateau known as South Pass begins. This trail over the Rocky Mountains is short on freshwater, but landmarks such as the four-hundred-foot-high Devil's Gate, towering above the narrow trail, provide inspirational viewing. Do not be distracted by the glittering gold specks lying in the creek beds. Simple tests will prove that this is worthless iron pyrite, commonly known as fool's gold.

## Shopping at Fort Hall

After South Pass, the trail divides. Travelers will want to take the northern route to Fort Hall, where a short spur leads to the California Trail. Here, nine hundred miles from St. Joseph, the long, difficult trek is nearly half over.

Fort Hall is a run-down wood and adobe structure. Small rooms contain various things for trade such as furs, food, and other items. The men who work here dress in animal skins, and many Indian lodges are located nearby for travelers to purchase ponies and skins. In addition, clothing may be washed here and letters can be posted. Letters will find their way to destinations in the East in three to four months' time.

## The Hated Humboldt

Heading westward again, travelers will find themselves following the slow-moving Snake River and crossing its many tributaries, some with great difficulty. The trail winds past eerily shaped lava towers, columns, pyramids, and minarets known as the City of Rocks. Again, hot and dusty conditions prevail, and the hard, flinty volcanic hills glisten in the sun.

As travelers enter the desert known as the Great Basin, they may look back fondly on their journey along the meandering Platte, no matter what hardships they have experienced. The only way through this primitive, barren wilderness is by tenaciously following the Humboldt, or "Humbug," River.

The Humboldt starts out fresh and cool, but as it snakes westward for a length of 350 miles, it becomes more of a creek than a river. Its milky, warm, salty, and sulfurous water is drinkable by only those with the strongest stomachs. Although the water may be too horrible to drink, it can be made into coffee, making it slightly more palatable. Animals might also be coaxed into drinking this foul-tasting brew.

Although water is scarce, the road here is solid and easy to travel. However, visitors must occasionally cross the river to avoid soft sand hills where wagons can be buried up to their axles. Dust storms are another problem along the Humboldt, and tornado-like "dust devils" may be seen from miles away. To avoid the worst of the dust, travel early in the morning and late in the day around sunset. Stay off the trail in the middle of the day when winds are strongest.

After thirty to sixty days along the "Humbug," emigrants are joyous to see the last of it when it simply disappears into the desert floor at a landmark known as the Humboldt Sink. Unfortunately, the Forty Mile Desert, also known as the "Valley of the Shadow of Death," awaits.

The desert trail crosses loose sand, sage-covered hills, plains, and alkali flats. The heat will test the patience of even the hardiest travelers. The water that is available along most of the trail is undrinkable. Travelers are advised to wait until the moon is growing full and cross the desert at night, putting as many miles

*The Humboldt River's water is salty and must be boiled before travelers can attempt to drink it.*

behind them as possible so that this part of the journey ends quickly and safely.

About twenty miles into the desert, several springs have water that is scalding hot. When cooled, this mineral-laden water is barely tolerable for drinking. After the springs, the road becomes soft and sandy, and the feet of your cattle may sink up to twelve inches in the ashy dust.

## Into the Mountains

After the Forty Mile Desert, travelers will begin the long, nearly perpendicular climb up Carson Pass. Where level ground may be found, visitors will see a welcome oasis of green trees and grasses along the Carson River. Following the river, the snow-capped Sierra Nevada rise three thousand feet above the wagon trains, providing a majestic sight to desert-weary travelers.

Although the scenery is beautiful, travelers need to negotiate Carson Pass at eighty-five hundred feet and then West Pass at ninety-five hundred feet. Even in August, evening frost and cold temperatures may weaken the strongest emigrants.

The trail follows the rough-and-tumble Carson River, and thousands of rocks and boulders hinder progress along the way. Fresh food, however, is available, with wild berries and deer in great abundance. Eat well, because it is necessary here to double-team the wagons; in other words, you need to hitch all available animals to one wagon, take it up a particularly steep portion of the trail, and then return for the next wagon. In some spots, it may be necessary to empty each wagon and lift it over huge boulders with pulleys and rope. William G. Johnston describes his frustrations with this difficult work in his 1849 book *Overland to California*. This feat was accomplished with "the most extraordinary profanity that ever saluted the ears, whether of dumb beasts or of men; indeed, the air seemed densely blue with oaths while all this was in progress. . . . The amount of labor required . . . was simply beyond conception."[2]

Finally, the trail winds down to Hangtown, or Placerville, one of the richest gold mining regions in the world. From there, it is downhill to Sutter's Fort, the site of the first gold discovery that caused thousands to take this great adventure.

# CHAPTER FOUR

# The Sea Route to Gold Country

Tourists living on the eastern or southern coasts of the United States might want to book passage to California aboard a ship. Every week, dozens of oceangoing vessels depart from large cities such as New York City, Boston, Baltimore, and New Orleans. The journey will take the visitor down the southern coast of the United States, then make stops in Panama; Rio de Janeiro, Brazil; and other cities before rounding Cape Horn at the southernmost tip of South America. Once headed north again, passengers can expect to visit ports of call in Lima, Peru; Panama City; Acapulco, Mexico; San Diego; and other cities. This method of travel is ideal for those who do not have the physical strength or the wherewithal to walk across the country.

The 13,328-mile sea route around Cape Horn is the time-honored method for reaching California, and has been used by whale hunters, traders, and travelers for centuries. Although this trip is lengthy and sometimes dangerous, the route has been well charted, so experienced sea captains can avoid the shipwrecks that befell earlier travelers. But, as author Fayette Robinson writes, this route is "a long voyage of indefinite length, of which no seamanship can make any promise. It can, however, scarcely occupy less than six months, and may occupy from six to twelve. The cost of this voyage will be, all told, about five hundred dollars."[3]

## The Sea-Land Route

There is a second, if less popular, route for travelers heading to California. Instead of staying aboard a ship for months as it rounds South America, tourists can disembark in Panama and then travel across the narrow isthmus by boat and on foot. Arriving at the Pacific Ocean on the western side of Panama, visitors may catch a northbound ship to take them to San Francisco.

Tourists choosing this route land in Chagres on the north side of Panama. From there, the distance to Panama City on the Pacific is only seventy-five miles. The first fifty miles of this journey is taken in fifteen- to twenty-five-foot-long native-style dugout canoes called *bungos*. Travelers must employ native boatmen to paddle and pole their *bungos* down the Chagres River. The trip cost only $10 in 1849, but it now has climbed to over $40, with some boatmen asking up to $100. Always offer the lowest price and bargain until you reach a satisfactory medium.

The trip down the Chagres can take less then thirty hours if the weather coop-erates. If it rains, it can take up to one week. Many dangers lurk in this tropical river. *Bungos* often become entangled in the rocks and branches strewn throughout the stream. Drunken passengers fall overboard and drown—or may be eaten by alligators. And the clouds of mosquitoes that suck blood also spread malaria. Even though it may be oppressively hot and humid, be sure to keep your skin covered to prevent these infernal insects from biting.

There are no hotels or restaurants in the Panamanian interior, so expect the roughest accommodations. Travelers here survive on a diet of baked monkey and

*Ships take travelers westward along the Panama route.*

*The land journey to California is rough and requires some mule travel.*

roasted iguana, along with tropical fruit such as lemons and oranges. At night, natives along the river rent (often filthy) hammocks for $2 apiece.

Once you have reached Cruces by boat, the final twenty-five miles are dense jungle and towering mountains. This journey, on muleback or on foot, may take two or three days.

Before the gold rush, Panama City consisted of little more than broken-down shacks and overgrown streets and plazas that were built by the Spanish in the seventeenth century. Today, the city is overrun with U.S. citizens, with dozens of hotels, restaurants, and grocery stores

that cater specifically to Americans. Prices are high here, and goods are two to three times more expensive than in the States. Flour, for instance, is $14 a barrel, and chickens $15 a dozen. Rough hotel rooms are available for the exorbitant price of $8 per night. Those wishing to save on hotel bills may pitch their tents in open spaces throughout the town.

The sea-land route through Panama is sometimes called the "Gamblers Route," because once you arrive in Panama City, finding passage north to San Francisco is uncertain. In the first year of the gold rush, almost ten thousand Americans found themselves stranded in Panama City with

*A native fishing boat arrives at its first stop on the Chagres River. Emigrants to California can hire such boats for their journey.*

only a handful of ships heading north. Today, that situation has been remedied somewhat, but travelers still must wait weeks or even months before finding a spot on a ship traveling north from Panama to California. And when ships finally do arrive, tickets are so scarce that bidding wars may ensue and prices may climb from $500 to $1,000. Sometimes, there is no space at any price. As Robinson warns,

It is fair to conclude that for a long time the steamers on both sides of the [Panama] Isthmus will be thronged, and very little comfort will be enjoyed. It must be remembered that

long delays are likely to ensue. . . . The passenger who leaves New York in a luxurious steamer will enter San Francisco, in all probability, amid the grease of a Nantucket whaler or the more disgusting filth of a Chilean or Peruvian [fishing boat], and the money which should be expended in researches in [gold country] will be wasted at Chagres or Panama.[4]

The final leg of this journey can take anywhere from twenty to sixty days depending on the weather. In this region, the Pacific is known for westerly winds that can sometimes push ships way off course, sometimes as far west as the Sandwich, or Hawaiian, Islands. Although these islands are known for their remarkable tropical splendor, this detour may add weeks to your journey.

## Booking a Ship

Whatever route you choose to take, you will need to book passage to leave the United States in late December. Although this may expose the ship to violent storms in the first days, summerlike weather will be the rule once the vessel nears the equator.

Travelers should be advised that the rush to gold country has created a great demand for ships, and almost every available ship, brig, schooner, and steamer has been pressed into service. Many of these worn-out, motley hulks were destined for the scrap heap before they were patched up, scrubbed out, and furnished with bunks to take advantage of the exorbitant ticket prices. Although all owners advertise that they run first-class passenger ships, some still reek of whale blubber, cattle, or even garbage from previous use. And recent reports indicate that 90 percent of ship captains lack the skills for making this long, treacherous journey. Thus, choose carefully before leaving port. Try to find a sober captain who has made the voyage a number of times.

Those who can afford it should book passage on clipper ships, the fastest vessels on the water today. Though this is the most expensive way to travel, clippers can make the journey from New York to San Francisco in a little over three months.

Those short of funds can look to other sources to raise money. For example, even stuffy East Coast bankers have caught gold fever. People with good credit may find willing lenders to lay out money for tickets in exchange for a percentage of future profits in the California goldfields.

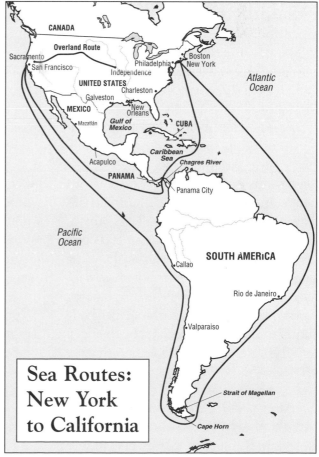

**Sea Routes: New York to California**

When booking passage aboard a ship, try to bargain for the best freight rate with the captain. You will want to bring mining gear packed in trunks, since it is much cheaper to buy tents, picks, shovels, firearms, gold scales, and other necessary equipment close to home. Beware, however, of con artists who are trying to sell all manner of fraudulent goods, such as "California Gold Grease," which purveyors falsely claim attracts gold when smeared on the skin.

## Around the Horn: The Good, the Bad, and the Ugly

Once the ship leaves the United States in late fall or early winter, the temperature should grow warmer with every passing day as the Atlantic trade winds keep the sails full with a fresh wind.

After a stop in Rio de Janeiro, temperatures begin to drop. This is a stormy part of the Atlantic, and rain, fog, and high winds make travel miserable. With temperatures dipping into the frigid 30-degree range, passengers will find themselves gathering belowdecks around coal- or wood-fired cast-iron stoves. Howling gales are common, and it is not unusual for huge waves to break over the ship, pouring down the hatches and soaking everybody and everything belowdecks. The rolling of the ship may create chaos as steamer trunks, wine bottles, food, dishes, stoves, and other items are tossed about.

After about a month of this difficult passage, the Falkland Islands will come into view. In this region, rain may turn to hail and snow and water casks may freeze. Expect conditions to continue to deteriorate as the ship rounds Cape Horn on the southernmost point of the journey, about one hundred days after leaving New York.

Once the ship begins to sail to the north, temperatures should begin rising into the 80-degree range. The icy storms of Cape Horn are forgotten as clear, blue skies and sunshine mark the days, broken only by occasional squalls and rain. After six months or so, passengers will lay over in Panama City, and before another month has passed, will be sailing through the Golden Gate into San Francisco.

## Seasickness

The most formidable enemies of the sea traveler on this journey are bad food and seasickness. With the ship rolling and pitching on rough seas, it is inevitable that, at any given moment, a significant percentage of the passengers—many of whom have never been to sea before—will be extremely seasick, nauseated, and vomiting. As Charles H. Williams recounts in the book *From New York to San Francisco via Cape Horn in 1849,*

[I] came very near being thrown out of my berth by the rolling of the ship repeatedly. . . . My slumbers were disturbed throughout the night by the crack of crockery and the falling of various articles, as well as by the vomiting of different passengers, who kept it up pretty regularly all night.[5]

## Food

Most ship lines promise to provide food during the journey, but these provisions often range from awful to inedible. Travelers have reported being served meals that consisted of rotten pork, beans swarming with maggots, and thick, hard biscuits filled with weevils. Even the dreadful food that does not crawl off on its own is frequently bland, greasy, and stale. Expect to be served a concoction known as lobscouse, a stringy hash of onions, hardtack biscuits, salt pork, water, and thickener. Another common dish is called Hushamagrundy—a stew of parsnips, turnips, and ground-up codfish.

*The ocean journey is often unpredictable and difficult.*

Fresh water is another problem for tourists. Water that has been stored in ship vats for months at a time develops an astonishingly rancid flavor that must be cut with vinegar or molasses to be made potable. Travelers should bring a healthy supply of brandy, whiskey, or rum, which can help make the water more drinkable. But cargo space is limited and shipping rates high, which prevents most passengers from bringing their own food and drink.

## Entertainment

Those not stricken with food poisoning and seasickness will find themselves fighting off boredom, since few passenger lines

# Meeting Neptune at the Equator

Sailors have developed many rituals over the centuries for celebrating notable shipboard events. One such ceremony that helps alleviate boredom on the New York to California route is performed when a ship crosses the equator. This rite is meant to initiate first-timers, called pollywogs, who are mercilessly teased by crew members, known as shellbacks, who have crossed the equator before.

The ceremony differs from ship to ship but typically involves sailors portraying mythical characters such as the pirate Davy Jones, and Neptune, the ancient Roman god of the sea. Sailors playing these roles make masks and ridiculous costumes specifically for the event, using pieces of seaweed, tablecloths, rope, and other odds and ends found laying about the ship.

When the play begins, Davy Jones orders the pollywogs to appear before King Neptune as the ship passes the equator. The pollywogs parade before the king and are charged with trumped-up crimes by crew members. For punishment, the pollywogs are given a symbolic baptism in a barrel of slimy water made ripe with fish guts and other horrible debris. At the end of the ceremony, music plays, bottles of liquor are passed around, guns are fired into the air, and the newly baptized shellbacks are given paper "certificates" by the captain to confirm their new status.

offer onboard entertainment. Some tourists do pack books, and these are often passed from one traveler to another until they fall to pieces from overuse. And don't forget to bring along a deck of cards or a checkerboard, chess set, backgammon board, or other games.

Those with an artistic bent may draw and paint. Intellectuals can meet in groups to discuss books, wildlife, and politics. And there are often amateur musicians onboard providing nightly songfests; passengers sing together to the accompaniment of violins, accordions, guitars, and flutes. Sportfishing breaks the boredom and also provides food for dinner, and playful schools of porpoises swimming alongside the ship provide sightseeing pleasures. There are also many stops along the way in exotic locations where new and exciting experiences await.

## Touring Rio de Janeiro

The first stop on the way to California, after about thirty days at sea, is usually Rio de Janeiro. Passengers will know they are within fifty miles of this first port of call when they see the awe-inspiring Sugar Loaf Mountain on the horizon.

Rio, with a population of about 250,000, is now teeming with many thousands of California-bound Americans eager for fresh food, water, liquor, and entertainment. Prices are low. An entire restaurant meal may be had for less than 50 cents. An overnight stay in a luxury hotel is around $5. No matter how fine the hotel, however, visitors can expect to have their sleep disturbed by a profusion of buzzing mosquitoes and scurrying roaches and rats.

The layover in Rio should be from ten to fourteen days. During this time, your ship captain will be reloading his vessel with food, water, and other necessities. Meanwhile, travelers will have many days to visit some of the fine attractions in Rio.

The botanical gardens will fascinate tourists who have an interest in tropical foliage. This ten-acre site contains luxuriant plants from around the world, including those that produce tea, cinnamon, cloves, and nutmeg. Tall palm trees line the avenues, and fruit trees such as lemon, breadfruit, plantain, and banana are found in abundance. Tours of the botanical garden are conducted by knowledgeable guides. Interpreters who understand both English and the native Portuguese may also be hired for a few dollars. Visitors will find restaurants near the botanical gardens with meals for about $2.

The central market is another Rio attraction. Here, visitors will find a variety of fruits and vegetables for sale, including garlic, onions, oranges, limes, bananas, figs, and extremely spicy cayenne peppers. Colorful birds for sale, such as parrots and canaries, and pet monkeys also provide novelty to visiting Americans.

## What to Do in Peru

After shipping out from Rio, travelers can expect many more weeks aboard their ship with little excitement save that provided by the weather, which becomes more extreme as the ship rounds Cape Horn.

The next major port of call is Callao, Peru, located about nine miles from Lima, which is high in the Andes Mountains on the western shore of South America. Lima, with a population of sixty thousand, is one of the oldest and richest cities in South America, and well worth the visit. The walled city is varied and interesting, containing magnificent churches, government buildings, hotels, and restaurants. At the Grand Plaza in the center of town, fine hotels such as the Grand Ball Hotel offer rooms for $2 a night and meals at reasonable prices. There are also several good theaters in Lima featuring plays and variety shows for as little as $1.

The streets of Lima are filled with women riding on donkeys and smoking cigars made from tobacco rolled in corn husks. These smokes are offered for sale and enjoyed by many tourists. As Franklin A. Buck writes in his 1850 book *A Yankee Trader in the Gold Rush*, "Everyone smokes and smokes everywhere; at the dinner table and at the hotel, even. I have been revelling in a cloud of smoke ever since I have been here."[6]

The central market in Lima offers a variety of high-quality tropical fruits, livestock, and exotic animals, as traveler Mark Hopkins writes:

After breakfast and mass, I went to the market place. . . . I spent an hour or so pleasantly in this place. It was crowded with all classes and sexes, not a few very pretty girls, who did not seem to be displeased at the ardent gazes of . . . Americans. They have a fine assortment of fruits of all kinds, peculiar to the tropics as well as apples, grapes, etc. The best fruit I have ever tasted I think are the cheremoya, which is magnificent. Then they have their meat market with a good variety attended almost altogether by women, a great many of whom are . . . dressed with their sleeves laced and dresses flounced. At the market you can buy all sorts of articles, as peddlers of all kinds spend their time here and spread all their goods out for public view.[7]

## Gold Ahead!

After clearing South America, ships will land at Panama City, and San Francisco's Golden Gate lies only weeks ahead. Many ships stop in the splendid towns of Acapulco, Mexico; San Diego; and Monterey, making the last part of the journey a festive affair. As the tropical air of Southern California gives way to the

## Sam Brannan

Sam Brannan arrived in San Francisco in 1846 and nearly single-handedly started the gold rush two years later when gold was discovered at Sutter's Fort. Brannan bought all the mining supplies he could find and put them up for sale in his trading post located in nearby Sutterville. In order to drum up business, Brannan traveled to the city and walked up and down the streets carrying a bottle of gold purportedly taken from the American River. Before long, a few people took Brannan's advice and headed up to gold country. A few lucky miners even returned to San Francisco as rich men, showing off small sacks of gold to gaping onlookers.

With such displays, gold fever hit San Francisco practically overnight, and nearly every man in town left the city in search of instant wealth. Businesses and houses were simply left empty as their owners ran off to the goldfields. San Francisco's only school closed, and the one teacher who worked there took his students to find gold along the American River.

Today, few travelers will find those legendary abandoned houses. Instead, emigrants will see a city that has grown in a few short years to include a population of more than fifty thousand. A nearly equal number pass through annually on their way to gold country.

gray skies above San Francisco Bay, passengers will be offered a fine view of the city. The harbor is filled with hundreds of ships whose masts are swaying in the wind like barren trees.

By the time the ship rolls into the bay, passengers will have spent almost two hundred days aboard the same ship, providing all went well. And their grand journey has only just begun. Once the vessel drops anchor, the mad rush is on to gather supplies and make travel arrangements into gold country via steamer up the Sacramento River.

San Francisco itself is a singularly exciting city. Tourists would be well advised to take in as many sights as possible and enjoy what the city by the bay has to offer. For after passing through the bustling streets of San Francisco, only the rough-and-tumble wilderness of gold country lay ahead.

# CHAPTER FIVE

# Touring San Francisco

San Francisco is the busy gateway to gold country, but the city barely existed in 1847, just four years ago. At that time, the sleepy village was called Yerba Buena and contained less than 450 people. The town had one hotel, a few bars, and a gristmill. The small village had grown up around the natural protected harbor, and when a ship sailed into the port once or twice a year, the entire town came out to greet it.

By 1849, Yerba Buena had been renamed San Francisco, gold had been discovered at Sutter's Fort, and the population had increased by more than 1,000 percent to include fifty-thousand permanent residents. These people have come from nearly every point on the globe, and many different languages are heard today on the city streets, including Chinese, English, French, German, Italian, Portuguese, Spanish, and Swedish.

There are currently about one thousand derelict ships in San Francisco Harbor that were abandoned by crews and captains in the heat of gold fever. Many of these worthless hulks have been converted to serve tourists. They are used as warehouses, restaurants, saloons, and hotels. The masts of these ships have been pounded into the shallow mud of Yerba Buena Cove to act as a foundation for the numerous wharves, piers, and shaky walkways that have been constructed to connect the ships. Meanwhile, the sails are being sold to visitors for tents. Travelers in need of instant housing can try to obtain a large piece of this sail canvas for shelter needs in gold country, but it may cost up to $30 for an eight-by-eight-foot square.

## Where to Stay: Hotels

Few towns in history have ever experienced the rapid growth that San Francisco witnessed. As a result, there is an extreme shortage of housing and hotel rooms in the city. Those with money to spare can pay up to $38 a week for a single room at the St. Francis Hotel. Others may find comfortable accommodations for around $28 a week at the Mark Hopkins Hotel (at five stories, this wood-and-stone landmark is the tallest building in the state).

## Dormitories

Those living on a shoestring budget may find a bed, known as a "flop," for $6 a week in a dormitory. Dormitories are often filled with as many as fifty other men. In some flophouses, bed space is so limited that men sleep in eight-hour shifts. As soon as one man rises from a bed, another lies down to take his place.

## The Tent City

A large tent city has been hastily built on one of San Francisco's highest perches, Telegraph Hill. It is so named because a telegraph station situated there informs citizens whenever a ship arrives in port so that they can rush down to the docks to pick up mail and supplies carried by the incoming vessels. In this area, accommodations may be obtained for pennies a day. A warning to tourists staying in the tent city: Wild animals such as grizzly bears, cougars, coyotes, and wolves roam the San Francisco hillsides and sometimes attack people. Keep a loaded firearm handy.

Although the tent city is a muddy mess of down-and-out miners, there are even worse places to sleep. The wharves

*Travelers will find inflated prices and crowded streets in San Francisco.*

provide housing for the poorest of visiters, who sleep under makeshift shelters constructed from bales of hay and straw.

## Where to Eat

Climbing hilly streets in search of shelter works up an appetite. Fortunately, a cornucopia of choices abounds in the city's restaurants. The traveler will find dishes both familiar and exotic, with establishments offering American, Chinese, French, German, Mexican, Russian, and Swedish cuisine.

In addition, the ocean, bay, and outlying hills provide a profusion of fresh, high-quality meats and seafood that would satisfy even the most demanding gourmet. These delicacies include abalone, antelope, bear, deer, duck, elk, goose, oysters, partridge, quail, rabbit, salmon, shrimp, trout, and turtle. Restaurants also offer the finest selection of wines and cigars.

*A word of advice for travelers:* Oysters and champagne are so popular among San Francisco diners that the oyster beds around the city have been completely depleted. Prices are exorbitant for the prized mollusks because they have to be shipped in from the north.

Although San Francisco's population is about 98 percent male, women run some of the finest restaurants. For example, Wilson's Hotel, run by Luzena Wilson, offers hearty meals for miners and other visitors. Travelers in search of a home-cooked Sunday morning breakfast will find a large number of miners lining up in front of this establishment.

San Francisco's ethnic neighborhoods offer a wide variety of foods from different nations. Adventurous tourists—or those longing for a meal from their home country—can travel to the city's ethnic enclaves for culinary excitement. Travelers searching for Italian or Spanish food should visit the North Beach neighborhood along Columbus Avenue. Irish food may be found on Market Street around St. Patrick's Cathedral. Visitors to the "Little China" neighborhood at the intersection of Sacramento and Dupont will find Asian cuisine, and those in search of seafood should visit the Portuguese fishermen at Rincon Point and Washerwoman's Bay.

The French have settled on Commercial Street near the Polka Saloon. French restaurants are highly recommended because, as traveler Hinton Helper writes in *Dreadful California,* "[The] French are better cooks, cleaner, more polite and attentive to their guests and less accustomed to adulterating their provisions."[8] Dinner in a French restaurant may be obtained for $2 per person; the addition of wine adds another $1 to $3 to the bill.

## Shopping for Food

While fresh meats and seafood are plentiful in the many markets throughout the city, travelers might want to beware of foodstuffs such as flour, butter, and common meats such as beef, pork, mutton, and chicken. These provisions are often shipped from the eastern states to California via Cape Horn.

# Fire Warning

Away from the piers, the majority of San Francisco's buildings are built from highly combustible Oregon pine. Fires are common—and deadly—occurrences. For example, in June 1851, the sixth major fire in three years raged through the city, leveling a ten-block area and damaging an additional six blocks. At this time, the Jenny Lind Theater burned to the ground for the second time in as many years. High winds and lack of water reserves aggravated the disaster. Plans are under way to require new buildings to use fireproof brick and iron shutters and doors, and to have water tanks installed on the roofs.

*San Francisco's great fire of 1851 sends people scurrying for safety.*

During their long journey, they must pass through the tropics twice, and the food often arrives in San Francisco sour, rancid, or rotten. These items will still be offered by shippers and merchants, however, who can still profit from their sale.

# Entertainment: Saloons

Many restaurants are attached to saloons, and these drinking establishments are the most profitable businesses in San Francisco. By the end of 1849, the city had over five hundred bars and taverns. The saloons light up the streets well into the night, and all kinds of music may be heard wafting from the doorways.

Though visitors might find shortages of everything from suspenders to fresh fruit, there is never a shortage of alcoholic libations. Although prices are high—first-class taverns charge an inflated 25 cents per drink—the average menu offers a wide range of beverages from around the world, including Irish whiskey, Holland gin, Jamaican rum, French wine, Portuguese port, French cognac, and so on. The local saloons also sell mixed drinks and try to outdo each other with amusing names for such beverages such as Eye Opener, Smasher, IOU, One-Eyed Joe, Ching Ching, Moral Suasion, Rooster Tail, Flip Flap, Old Sea Dog, and Stone Wall.

Travelers should be warned, however, that San Francisco has no hospitals or police stations to help those in trouble. Crime is rampant, and roving street gangs occasionally terrorize the town. The best way to remain safe is to travel in groups.

## Gambling

There are no restrictions on who may operate a gambling parlor in San Francisco, so

*San Francisco's casinos offer gamblers a variety of games of chance, including many card games.*

there are hundreds of such establishments, many attached to saloons.

Even for the nongambler, it is worth visiting one of San Francisco's finer casinos if only to view the huge mirrors, crystal chandeliers, life-sized paintings, and engravings of nude women that adorn the walls. Bars and tabletops are made from the finest marble and set with silver and cut-glass goblets and chiseled vases full of fresh flowers. Floors are also marble, while ceilings are decorated with painted frescoes like those found in European cathedrals. String quartets and brass bands entice passersby into the casino while elegantly dressed prostitutes ply the carpeted aisles offering their services to winners. Among the favorite games in San Francisco's gambling dens are poker, roulette, faro, and three-card monte.

The El Dorado on Portsmouth Square and the Arcade on Commercial Street are San Francisco's most renowned gambling parlors. Many smaller establishments attempt to imitate the glittering accoutrements found in these places. Despite their outward appearance, the upscale casinos do not discriminate between rich and poor customers, and tourists on any budget are welcome. Bags of gold dust, however, are usually not allowed for betting at the finer establishments. Instead, patrons are asked to exchange their raw gold for coins. The exchange rates paid by casinos, however, are often very unfair, so it is a good idea for travelers to change their gold into coinage at banks or assay houses.

Small casinos, however, will take gold nuggets, and it is not unusual to see a card dealer pulling out a scale and test kit to analyze a miner's precious metal. *A word of warning:* Those who try to plump up their gold piles with brass filings or other filler may find themselves staring down the business end of a large revolver.

Profits are high at gambling halls, and there is a fierce competition to attract visitors. Look for a gambling parlor that offers free food and liquor to its patrons. Some parlors display large sums of money in glass cases—as much as $20,000—in order to entice hopeful gamblers to their tables. But beware, the gaming tables in most casinos are rented to professional gamblers, who often cheat tourists out of their money. As Helper writes, "Every possible variety of gaming that can be accomplished by cards and dice is practiced here and every false and dishonest trick is resorted [to] to fleece ignorant men of their money."[9]

## Other Forms of Entertainment

Almost all saloons, gambling dens, restaurants, and hotels offer live performances. Singers, comedians, and actors perform on stages or even on pool tables pushed together. Popular child entertainers dress in the native costumes of their homelands and dance traditional dances while other children play music. Musicians play folk music from faraway countries to cheer up homesick miners. French music may be heard at Café Chantants on Commercial, while German songs are regularly sung at the Thistle Inn on Broadway.

Immigrant women from Central and South America provide some of the most sought-after entertainment in the city. In various hotels and barrooms, these talented dancers perform the popular Fandango dance to the applause of mostly male audiences.

The streets also bustle with all forms of music by way of street singers. Strolling orchestras and organ grinders may be found on any corner, some drawing rather large, boisterous crowds.

## Shakespeare Conquers the West

Almost as soon as gold was discovered in California, hundreds of New York actors packed their theatrical trunks with costumes and play scripts and headed West, where eager audiences awaited them.

The most popular playwright in California is sixteenth-century Englishman William Shakespeare. Perennial favorites such as *Hamlet, Macbeth, Othello, Romeo and Juliet*, and *The Tempest* may be found in various San Francisco playhouses throughout the year.

The first professional actors performed Shakespeare in San Francisco in 1850 on a hastily constructed stage built in a theater that housed a circus. Before long, however, gaily decorated theaters such as the Jenny Lind, Washington Hall, the American, Maguire's Opera House, and the Metropolitan opened their doors. Since that time, famous actors such as

Julia Deane Hayne, James Stark, Barney Williams, Lola Montez, Laura Keene, and James E. Murdoch have all been performing in the city's theaters.

That high-quality actors have come to San Francisco is hardly surprising since producers pay their top talent as much as $3,000 per week—a veritable fortune unavailable to all but the luckiest miners. And even less gifted actors may earn up to $1,000 a week. Nevertheless, actors who are planning to emigrate to the city should remember that expenses are high and folly common. Stark, for example, lost a fortune in a silver-mine scam, and McKean Buchanan forfeited nearly $20,000 in a single poker game.

Nonactors will find the theater a welcome respite from the often harsh realities of daily life in the city. Production companies spare no expense in producing painted backdrops of landscapes, palaces, and other scenes. Offstage, soundmen rattle iron, shake peas in cans, and pound drums to simulate thunderstorms. Actors appear onstage dressed in colorful costumes, wigs, and makeup.

In total, San Francisco theaters put on about one thousand shows a year, including nine hundred plays. But tourists wanting to attend these productions should obtain tickets early. When the Olympic Amphitheater opened in February 1850, the production of *Othello* sold out within hours.

Travelers not given over to Shakespeare will find other theatrical entertainment such as Rowe's Olympic Circus, featuring the minstrel music of the Ethiopian Serenaders.

## Other Services

There is no shortage of lawyers, doctors, or dentists in San Francisco (as well as plen-

ty of quacks and criminals posing as professionals). With sickness and epidemics all too common, doctors are charging extravagant rates and making fortunes, even though the cures offered by most have done little to stop the tide of disease. You can expect to pay one ounce of gold (about

*Carriages await weary travelers on the street bordering Portsmouth Square, San Francisco's first town square and the hub of the city.*

$16) to obtain the services of these professionals.

In addition, the streets of San Francisco are rife with jewelry stores of every kind, most selling pins, rings, and other goods fashioned from California's native gold and gems. These items are purchased by miners who send them home to mothers, sisters, sweethearts, and wives.

In conclusion, there is something for everybody in San Francisco. There is little doubt that, in the coming years, the city by the bay will continue to grow, flourish, and prosper.

# CHAPTER SIX

# Touring Sacramento

I n 1839, John Sutter built his little fort on the American River, about two miles from where it flowed into the Sacramento River. At that time, the area was wilderness. No one could have envisioned the booming city of Sacramento that would be built virtually overnight after a pea-sized nugget of gold was found near Sutter's Mill in 1848.

After this discovery, Sutter wanted to build a city (humbly called Sutterville) at the site of his fort, in an area less prone to flooding. But mining merchant Sam Brannan had already opened his store next to the Sacramento River in an abandoned steamboat that was beached along the shore. Although Brannan's store was the only building in Sacramento at that time, the merchant had title to a large quantity of surrounding land, and he saw a way to make a fortune in real estate if the city was built nearby.

*Gold was first found on John Sutter's land in 1848.*

Brannan, working with Sutter's son John Jr., laid out the town at the confluence of the Sacramento and American Rivers against the wishes of Sutter Sr. Meanwhile, Brannan and John Jr. also invented the

name Sacramento to replace the town's old name of New Helvetia.

The location chosen by Brannan is scenic and inviting. The river here is nearly half a mile wide and the water is perfectly clear and fresh. As the distant ocean tides shift, the Sacramento's waters rise and fall two to three feet. The city itself is built on a wide plain of alluvial soil deposited by the river and worn flat by countless floods. Oaks and native grasses color the area a beautiful green, and the snow-capped peaks of the Sierra Nevada can be seen jutting skyward in the distance.

Sacramento was chartered in September 1849, and by this time the population had mushroomed to ninety-five hundred. The boomtown, however, was put to the test in January 1850 when (as the elder Sutter had predicted) a massive flood wiped out the entire town. The scene is described by author Franklin Street:

> Sacramento . . . was entirely inundated. . . . The rivers rose suddenly in the night, and before any person was aware of the fact, the water was rushing through the city in torrents; and soon was several feet deep, over the whole town. By very great exertions, the inhabitants were nearly all saved. But gloom and desolation prevailed throughout, even after the flood disappeared; and great distress followed—provisions became scarce and very high [in price]; and many were left without shelters to shield them from the inclemency of the weather.[10]

The city has since been completely rebuilt and remains a fascinating area with lots of history.

## Getting There from San Francisco

The Sacramento River provides a safe and easy route from San Francisco to Sacramento. Visitors must first sail to the northern reaches of San Francisco Bay and catch a steamer upriver to the "embarcadero" at the port of Sacramento. Six to eight boats make the one-hundred-mile trip every day. The journey takes eight to ten hours (on a good day) and costs an astronomical $10 to $30. Although these prices may seem high, many of these boats are of the highest quality—fast, comfortable, and splendidly decorated.

## The Streets of Sacramento

Although Sacramento was built hurriedly, unlike in San Francisco, planners charted out the city with wide, spacious streets. These pleasant avenues are named after letters of the alphabet, with A Street being farthest from the river and Z Street closest. Cross streets are numbered. J Street is the busiest street, occupied by stores, hotels, bakeries, casinos, and so on. K Street is the place for livestock auctions, and Front Street, which parallels the river, is crowded with a half-mile of business establishments.

## Commerce

A survey taken in late 1850 cataloged Sacramento's moneymaking ventures.

According to the survey, there were nearly 500 businesses in the city, including 80 clothing merchants, 65 blacksmith shops, 90 doctor offices, 70 law offices, and 100 flour and grain mills. Thirsty visitors will be glad to find 2 soda manufacturers, 3 lemon syrup makers, and 2 beer breweries. There are also 7 churches of various denominations in the burgeoning city.

## Shopping

Although the streets overflow with merchandise, don't expect any bargains. Most goods offered for sale must be brought upstream from San Francisco, and many originated on the East Coast. As a result, products cost from two to four times more

than they would on the Atlantic coast. The prices of some items are even higher. Eggs are selling for $1 to $3 apiece; apples, $1 to $5; coffee, $5 a pound; a butcher knife, $30; and boots, $100 a pair. So, while a lucky miner might make about $8 a day, he might still have trouble meeting his basic needs at these prices.

Wise shoppers might keep their eyes open for bargains at businesses teetering on the edge of bankruptcy. There is fierce competition here and many more merchants than business demands. Occasionally, goods may be purchased at fire-sale prices. But let the buyer beware—there are many merchants selling ridiculously overpriced junk. As traveler Hinton Helper so

*People visit on Sacramento's spacious streets.*

eloquently states, finding "instances of per-fidy and dishonesty in California merchants would be like taking inventory of blades of grass in a meadow."[11]

## Getting Around

Those wishing to get around Sacramento in style can buy a riding horse for about $110 from local Indians. Each animal comes complete with saddle, bridle, and spurs. This is the favorite mode of trans-portation in the city, as carriages are scarce.

Visitors who want to visit the dig-gings will find it easy to book passage on stagecoaches, which run three times a week to Stockton and most major towns.

Tourists wishing to ship freight to gold country can negotiate with the dri-vers of mule trains. These pack trains, some consisting of up to sixty mules har-nessed together, leave daily for the dig-gings. Prices vary as to goods shipped, space available, and other logistics.

*Carriages are costly and scarce in Sacramento.*

# Where to Stay

Dozens of hotels have sprung up in Sacramento, and, as in San Francisco, quality varies greatly. Most hotels are shoe-string operations dedicated to housing tourists and making a few extra dollars with stables and storage. They advertise with crudely made canvas signs—some quite amusing—that say things such as "Tip-top Accommodations for Man and Beast" and "Rest for the Weary and Storage for Trunks."[12]

The nicest hotel in town is the City Hotel, recently built by Brannan. This three-story building is grandly decorated with wrought-iron rails and large rooms that rent for $21 a week. As for the rest of the city's hotels, those who thought San Francisco's accommodations were primitive will be startled by what they find here. Most Sacramento hotels are simply dormitories where up to twenty drunken, snoring men may be found sleeping on any given night. They bed down on straw-stuffed cots that are covered with filthy coarse blankets that, in all likelihood, have never seen the wet side of a washboard. Guests usually sleep in their clothes, some even wearing their overcoats and muddy boots. In the morning, a single wash pan is offered for all guests, along with a single towel that, like the blankets, has never been washed.

Travelers can expect to find these flophouses crawling with bed bugs, cockroaches, rats, and other vermin. Human parasites also haunt the hotels, stealing money, clothing, and other items from those too trusting—or ignorant—to sleep with their valuables under their pillows.

The ragged village of makeshift housing that surrounds Sacramento is almost as large as the city itself. Here, visitors may also be found living in—or under—wagons, boxes, crates, cabins, and tents. The air hangs heavy with wood smoke from campfires, and the nostrils are assaulted with the odors of butchered meat, rotting fish, and unwashed humanity. A bottle of whiskey, however, may buy a visitor sleeping accommodations in some primitive bivouac or another.

On the other hand, those wishing to stay longer in Sacramento may want to simply construct their own home in the tent city. Be warned, however, that any piece of material that may be used to construct a shelter, such as muslin, canvas, old sails, logs, boards, sheet iron, tin, and even old packing crates, commands the highest of prices.

# What to Eat

Most of the cheap hotels in Sacramento offer dinner for $1; better establishments charge up to $2. Again, canvas signs will help inform prospective patrons of the nature of the business. Some of these signs read, "Good Fare, and Plenty of It," "Eating is done here," "Come in the Inn, and take a Bite," and "Replenish the Stomach in our House."[13]

For those travelers hoping to pinch pennies, the placid Sacramento River abounds with fish, especially salmon, which can grow up to five feet in length.

## Buying Food from the Natives

*While merchants charge top dollar for food-stuffs, savvy traders may obtain a wide variety of food from Sacramento's Native American population, as Edwin Bryant explains in his 1848 book* What I Saw in California.

This morning we were visited by numerous Indians from the neighboring *rancherias* [ranches], who brought with them watermelons, muskmelons, and strings of pan-fish, taken from a small pond about half a mile distant, with a sort of hand-trap. The Indians wade into the pond with their traps in hand, and take with them the fish, sometimes by dozens at a haul. These they wished to trade for such small articles as we possessed, and the cast-off clothing of the members of our party. Some of these Indians were partially clothed, others were entirely naked, and a portion of them spoke the Spanish language. They exhibited considerable sharpness in making a bargain, holding their wares at a high valuation, and although their desire to trade appeared to be strong, they would make no sacrifices to obtain the articles offered in exchange for them. But such was the desire of our men to obtain vegetables, of which they had been for so long a time deprived, that there was scarcely any article which they possessed, which they would refuse to barter for them.

## Entertainment: Theater

Although San Francisco may have the nicest theaters, Sacramento is home to the first theater in the state. The Eagle Theater opened in the autumn of 1849. Those who are familiar with the beautiful theaters of Broadway in New York, however, should not expect the same in Sacramento. The Eagle is a round canvas building topped with a tin roof. Although it looks exactly like the gambling parlor called the Round Tent next door, a crude sign designates it as a theater. Despite the shabby appearance, the theater cost an enormous $30,000 to build because of the inflated costs of construction materials needed to build the rows of wooden seats.

The Eagle Theater's colorful curtain portrays purple mountains, a yellow sky, and dark brown trees. Good seats in the box tier cost $3 per ticket, and this section accommodates about one hundred patrons. Cheaper seats in the pit are $2 and about three hundred people may be seated in these rows. It is advised that the traveler arrive early and pay the extra dollar for the box-tier seats because the outer rows border the canvas walls and, on stormy nights, patrons may be drenched with rain.

People take their entertainment where they can get it in Sacramento, and the Eagle Theater does brisk business. Visitors can determine whether they want to spend their hard-earned money on the shows after reading the following review of a recent play, *The Spectre of the Forest,* written by critic Stephen Massett:

The orchestra consisted of the fiddle— a very cheezy [instrument], played by a gentleman with one eye—a big drum, and a triangle, that served the double purpose of ringing in the boarders to their meals at the restaurant next door.[14]

New York correspondent Bayard Taylor also offers comments on the play and the audience-pleasing performance of Mrs. Henry Ray, an actress from New Zealand:

The interest of the play is carried to an awful height by the appearance of two [ghosts], clad in mutilated tent-covers, and holding . . . candles in their hands. At this juncture Mrs. Ray rushes in and [stands on one leg with the other raised and bent at the knee] . . . why she does it, no one can tell. This movement, which she repeats several times in the course of the three acts, has no connection to the tragedy; it is evidently introduced for the purpose of showing the audience that there is, actually, a female performer. The miners, to whom the sight of a woman is not a frequent occurrence, are delighted with these passages and applaud vehemently.[15]

# Gambling

As in San Francisco, gambling parlors provide the main entertainment to Sacramento's mostly male population. The newest casino, See's Exchange on Front Street, is also the brightest and best in the city. Opened in 1850, See's is in a building 120 feet long and 40 feet wide. The 15-foot-high ceilings are hung with fine chandeliers, and the walls display beautiful paintings of mountain scenery and partially clothed ladies. The parlor also boasts a house orchestra, two liquor bars, sixteen monte tables, two roulette wheels, two faro tables, and various other gaming tables.

The nearby Empire Casino rivals See's for opulence and entertainment. The three saloons in this gambling parlor are packed nearly every night, and the manager hires only the best musicians for the house band. A grand dance hall, which covers the entire second floor of the building, is located above the Empire. Tourists visiting Sacramento on major holidays such as the Fourth of July and New Year's Eve can attend grand balls in this hall, which are open to the public. Formal wear, however, is required, and those not sporting the finest tuxedos and evening gowns will be refused admission.

# Indian Entertainment

Those who are tired of losing at the card and roulette tables may find entertainment at the Indian camps. Their unique form of gambling is described by traveler Edwin Bryant:

They [Indians] are [seasoned] gamblers, and those who have been so fortunate as to obtain clothing, frequently stake and part with every rag upon their backs. The game which they most generally play is carried on as follows. [The players] seat themselves cross-legged on the ground, in a circle. They are then divided into two parties, each of which has two champions or players. A ball, or some small article, is placed in the hands of the players on one side, which they transfer from hand to hand with such sleight and dexterity that it is nearly impossible to detect the changes. When the players holding the balls make a particular motion with their hands, the antagonist players guess in which hand the balls are at the time. If the guess is wrong it counts one in favor of the playing party. If the guess is right, then it counts one in favor of the guessing party, and the balls are trans-

## Fourth of July Celebrations

When visiting Sacramento during the Fourth of July holiday, tourists can expect grand celebrations. This is one of the few days of the year that miners refuse to work and the streets are crowded with bearded prospectors in their flannel shirts, floppy hats, and boots.

During this patriotic celebration, Sacramento's streets are festooned with flags and red, white, and blue bunting. Tourists can expect the day to start out with a formal reading of the Declaration of Independence, possibly by a local man dressed in a Revolutionary War costume. This solemn and inspiring moment is usually followed by a parade featuring marching bands, veterans, the town's wealthiest citizens, and ladies dressed in all their finery.

After the parade, eating and drinking commences at neighborhood picnics with beer, potato salad, ham, turkey, and other fixings. Anyone bringing a bottle or a food contribution is usually welcome to join.

The bars and saloons begin to fill as night falls, and the citizens of Sacramento plan at least one grand ball, usually held at the City Hotel or above the Empire Casino. This event may attract as many as five hundred men and women dressed in their finest clothes. Those not attending the ball fill the streets and celebrate by shooting guns in the air and lighting firecrackers. Drunken revelry often leads to fights or even murders.

Tourists should get plenty of rest the day before the Fourth of July. Festivities may last until dawn or even through the next night.

ferred to them. The count of the game is kept with sticks. During the progress of the game, all concerned keep up a continual monotonous grunting, with a movement of their bodies to keep time with their grunts. The articles which are staked on the game are placed in the centre of the ring.[16]

Other Indian pastimes may be of interest to those travelers curious about California's native cultures. Bryant describes one such event that he witnessed:

There was a large gathering at the *rancheria* [Indian camp] . . . to celebrate some event. Dancing, singing, loud shouting, and howling, were continued without intermission the whole night. One of their [entertainments] consisted in fixing a scalp upon a pole and dancing around it, accompanying the dance with, at first, a low melancholy howl, then with loud shrieks and groans, until the performers appeared to become frantic with excitement.[17]

## A Growing City

Whether watching Indian ceremonies or the antics of New Zealand actresses, tourists in Sacramento may expect to have a pleasant visit, providing they are not caught there during plagues, floods, or fires. There is a spirit of camaraderie among visitors to the town—for many miners, it is the closest thing to civilization they see all year. And there is little doubt that Sacramento will have a long, illustrious future. There is even talk today that Sacramento might soon become the capital of California.

# CHAPTER SEVEN

# Touring Gold Country

By 1850, at least thirty towns had been established to answer to the needs of the miners in gold country. These miners spend, on average, two to three weeks at a time at the diggings and then journey to towns for supplies, drinks, gambling, and entertainment.

Most mining towns are very primitive—some are only tent towns—but many are growing at a rapid rate. While some of these towns may prosper and grow after the gold in the surrounding hills is exhausted, many will, no doubt, disintegrate into ghost towns as rapidly as they were built.

The towns are located in two regions: the northern gold country and the southern. Sacramento is the jumping-off spot for towns in the north, which include Placerville, Sutterville, Nevada City, and Marysville. The booming town of Stockton serves the southern towns of Bear Valley, Sonora, Angels Camp, and others.

## Getting to the Towns

To get to the towns in gold country, visitors will want to catch one of the dozens of fast coaches out of Sacramento or Stockton. The drivers are called "whips," and the stagecoaches are called Concord coaches because they were built in Concord, New Hampshire, and transported around "the Horn" by ship. The bright red Concords are decorated with yellow trim and travel at speeds of eight to ten miles an hour. They feature heavy front-to-rear leather suspension straps that cushion riders from the bumps and jolts of gold country's rough roads.

Coach companies offer wide-ranging service throughout the region. Expect coaches to carry six to nine passengers inside and on top. While riding, travelers will meet miners, gamblers, merchants, entertainers, and even a few women. The scenery is often beautiful as the wagons roll by bluffs, canyons, and valleys. At times, however, the journey becomes one of fear and awe as the coaches roll along steep mountain paths where a misstep by the horse team could result in a plunge a thousand feet down into a ravine. In addition, robbers and highwaymen sometimes haunt the roads, eager to separate travelers from their gold.

Coaches transport only people, packages, mail, and a small amount of personal luggage. Those wishing to transfer mining tools, building materials, and other heavy goods should hire space on a freight wagon. Often referred to as "land schooners," these huge wagons are built with wheels up to eight feet in diameter. Their drivers sit more than twelve feet above the ground.

These wagons can transport up to six tons of freight, using teams of six to eight mules. Finding space for hire on such a behemoth should not be too difficult. An estimated twenty-five thousand land schooner trips were completed from Sacramento in 1850 alone.

## Gold Country Towns: Marysville

Marysville, formerly known as Yubaville, is located due north of Sacramento, near the confluence of the Yuba and Feather Rivers. It is the main transfer point for goods and people arriving by steamer from Sacramento. Nine steamboats a day

*Prospectors wash gold in the Sierra foothills. Panning is a slow and tedious process but can sometimes yield big finds.*

service the area, with passenger tickets costing $20. Meals are served onboard for $1.50, and freight is 8 cents a pound.

From Marysville, stagecoaches and freight wagons service towns in the northernmost reaches of gold country. Teamsters, whips, and muleteers (mule drivers) fill the streets with their curses and shouts as they load and strap down heavy equipment or attempt to discipline their stubborn mule teams. Saloons are overflowing with colorful teamsters fortifying themselves with whiskey for the hard journey that lays ahead. Expect to find three mules for every person in Marysville, since estimates say that there are forty-five hundred of the hairy beasts and only fifteen hundred of the human variety.

Marysville has many businesses, including stores, hotels, bakeries, gambling dens, and a weekly local newspaper. Although there is no gold around Marysville, its banks are overflowing with deposits from miners in the area. As a regional hub, the quality of this town's food and lodging rivals that of Sacramento.

Travelers to Marysville can stay in a boardinghouse named the United States Hotel for $4 a day. Other hotels include the Tremont and the Atlantic. Restaurants offer inexpensive meals consisting of liver, steak, lamb, potatoes, soup, and bread.

# Nevada City

Nevada City, located about fifty miles from Marysville, is the fourth largest town in California. The trail from Nevada City to Sacramento is probably the best road in the state and is constantly crowded with stagecoaches and freight wagons.

Located on Deer Creek, the town is surrounded by mines with seemingly infinite riches. Nevada City was jump-started in 1849 when large quantities of gold were discovered in Little Deer Creek and Gold Run. Rumors spread that miners were pulling a pound of gold a day from these waterways, and a large number of prospectors flooded into the area. Soon, another great gold find was exposed at the Coyota diggings. At that time, there were fewer than six buildings in Nevada City, but the following spring a building boom ensued. As a result, there are now more than 100 stores, 35 hotels, 15 bakeries, 6 plush gambling dens, and hundreds of other various dwellings, including brothels and opium dens.

A steam-powered sawmill here produces over two thousand feet of lumber every day, and this output is expected to continue well into the future. Unfortunately, this lumber is highly flammable. In March 1851, about two hundred homes worth $1 million were destroyed in a conflagration here. Despite such dangers, at least four thousand people now inhabit the town, with an equal number camped out at mines in the surrounding hills. Local officials expect the population to soon reach ten thousand in Nevada City itself.

# Placerville

Placerville, located on a tributary of the American River, is the hub for the central

# How Hangtown Got Its Name

*In* California in 1850 Compared to What It Was in 1849, with a Glimpse at Its Future Destiny, *Franklin Street explains how Hangtown got its name.*

An old man in the neighborhood had, by dint of hard labor, accumulated some six thousand dollars in gold dust, a fact of which three villainous ruffians had become appraised, and learning that he lived in a tent by himself, they sought an opportunity to rid him of his valuable treasure. Approaching his tent, they discovered him apparently asleep, and he, learning from unguarded expressions which they let fall, that it was their intention to murder him if he should awake and discover them in the theft, he retained his exact position, with his eyes closed, until they had got possession of the sacks of gold, and fled in search of a safe retreat. One of the number remained to watch the movements of the old man until the others had time, as he thought, to make good their escape. But they were soon pursued, caught, and the dust found with them, which had been snugly put up in little buckskin sacks that were recognised by many who had seen them before. A formal court was then called, composed of miners in the neighborhood, and the three ruffians tried, condemned, and sentenced to be hung, which sentence was immediately executed by hanging on the limb of a large oak tree, which yet stands in the streets of Placerville, a monument to the tragical scene.

*Gold nuggets were unearthed under this street in Placerville, California.*

gold country transportation network. The town is about sixty miles from Sacramento, and a good coach driver can make the journey in eight hours.

Placerville has had several names, but it was originally known as Old Dry Diggings, because its streams dried up in the summer months. It later acquired the name Hangtown because any criminal convicted of murder could expect to be swinging by the neck from a tree in a matter of thirty minutes.

Placerville is located between two steep hills, and the streets extend for about a mile through the narrow valley. Lumber is plentiful in the region, and the town is a hodgepodge of log cabins and board buildings, none more than two stories high.

The surrounding mines were some of the first discovered in California. In the first two years of the gold rush, $2 million worth of gold was easily removed from surface mines here. In fact, a local woman found a sixteen-pound nugget of gold in her yard and surprised her husband at dinner by presenting it to him in her skillet. Since that time, miners have dug for gold just about everywhere in Placerville, even in the middle of Main Street, severely hampering mule teams and other transportation. They also dig in their cabin floors and in the steep hills and ravines; they even pluck gold dust out of the mortar used as building foundations. The obsession to find gold is so strong, in fact, that at a local funeral, miners standing around the dead man's grave saw glitter-ing gold dust in the freshly turned earth and the funeral had to be postponed while the hole was examined.

Despite all its gold, Placerville offers few accommodations to travelers. The El Dorado Hotel, a dowdy two-story cabin, rents rooms, and rough lodging may be obtained in rooms behind grocery stores and taverns. The El Dorado also has a restaurant serving pork and beans. Some local women sell home-baked goods to hungry miners. One such notable cook is Lucy Stoddard Wakefield, who sells more than 240 pies a day for $1 each directly from her cabin kitchen.

The most famous dish in town is the Hangtown Fry, an omelette made from eggs, bacon, and oysters. It was first concocted when a rich miner walked into the El Dorado and asked for their most expensive dish. Since the oysters were canned in Boston, eggs were scarce, and bacon scarcer, the chef whipped up the Hangtown Fry, which can now be obtained in finer restaurants in San Francisco and gold country.

Besides the El Dorado, one of the most popular establishments in Placerville is the house of prostitution owned by a young madam from New Orleans. Here, about a dozen women from the Sandwich Islands entertain men for about $50 a night. The madam is said to be worth $100,000 after only one year in business.

## Stockton

Stockton, originally called Mudville, is the most important city in the southern

*The El Dorado Hotel is a commodious and sophisticated resting spot for the weary tourist.*

gold region. The town was founded in 1849 by German immigrant Charles M. Weber, who obtained forty-nine thousand acres of land through a Spanish land grant. Weber tried to make his fortune by mining, but soon realized that it was much more profitable to sell land to forty-niners who were flooding into the city. Weber decided to call the town Stockton after Commodore R.F. Stockton, who commanded the naval forces in California during the Mexican War.

The town is situated on the banks of the San Joaquin River and has grown to be the third largest city in California in terms of size, commerce, and wealth. Banks within the city overflow with deposits of gold taken from all the southern mines. About six to seven thousand people inhabit Stockton, which sits on high ground amid the boggy, wet soil of the San Joaquin Valley, lands too low and wet to farm.

As in many mining towns, few women live in Stockton. There are fewer than three women per every one hundred men. The town has become a resort of sorts for long-haired, bearded miners taking a break from gold prospecting at nearby camps such as Fleatown, Cut Eye, Sucker Flat, Humbug Canyon, and Port Wine. These men stream into Stockton, especially when the weather turns cold in autumn, to bathe, cut their hair, eat a good meal, drink, gamble, and visit the local brothel. Visitors to Stockton can expect to compete for food and lodging with this rush of thrill seekers.

## Sonora

The town of Sonora, consisting of about four thousand people, sits in the middle of some of the richest gold regions in California. In fact, all the hills and valleys surrounding the town have been dug, scraped, shoveled, poked, and probed by miners searching for riches.

Originally founded by Mexican and Chilean miners, Sonora is about fifty miles southeast of Stockton and can be easily reached from that city by stagecoach. According to writer Hinton Helper, the journey is far from scenic:

Starting early in the morning, we travel as fast as a dare-devil driver can make four horses convey us. A

## Dancing the Fandango

*Those looking for entertainment in gold country might want to consider attending a Fandango, a Mexican ball named after the fandango, a rapid-paced dance in triple time. In* A Yankee Trader in the Gold Rush, *Franklin A. Buck describes the scene at one such event.*

The only dancing I have indulged in [in California] was at a fandango at the Sonorian Camp, three miles from here. It is a regular Mexican town, some 3000 people and about 40 houses and a number of Mexican families engaged in packing mules. . . .

Well, I heard of the fandango and I went. It was held in a good-sized room with a bar on one side, of course, and crowded with men and women, all smoking. The orchestra consisted of two fiddles and guitars and made pretty good music. The men were dressed in sky-blue velvet pants, open at the sides and rows of buttons, with white drawers, red sash and a fancy shirt. The Senoritas, with white muslin dresses . . . and silk stockings, looked very pretty. We [danced] cotillions and waltzes and one Senorita danced a fancy dance and made more noise with her little feet and slippers than I could with thick boots. She told me it was the "Valse Alleman.". . . Their cotillions are the same as ours except that the last figure is "alt promenade to the Bar," where you and your fair partner imbibe.

The Fandango went off well. I was very much amused and came away without being stabbed, which is lucky as such things often happen.

part of the country over which our road leads us is an elevated plain. Entirely destitute of trees and other vegetable products, it presents a most dreary and uninviting prospect. We see nothing around us but the naked earth. There is no accommodation for either bird nor beast—no resting-place for the one, nor food for the other.[18]

Sonora is built on a long, sloping hill and contains only one street, making the city about one mile long and only several hundred feet wide. All manner of tents, shacks, and shanties have been thrown up willy-nilly along this one main drag.

The best "hotel" in Sonora, typical of many in the mining region, is an unnamed, hastily constructed shack made from saplings and sticks woven together and covered with a patchwork of canvas sails. Tables, bunk beds, and benches are set on a dirt floor and guests eat, sleep, get drunk, smoke cigars, and play cards in the one large, undivided room. Each bunk contains five levels of flea-ridden wooden planks. These are covered with two-foot-wide, straw-stuffed mattresses and dirty blankets. Men sleep fully clothed but remove their hats.

Sleeping may be quite difficult in this situation, as the night is punctuated by angry shouts, fistfights, the moans of the sick, snoring, drunken retching, and curses. Some guests stuff cotton rags or bottle corks in their ears to obtain some rest.

The clamor usually dies down around 4:00 A.M. just as the early risers are getting up. The proprietors provide a water basin and single towel for the guests, and a line forms early to partake of this "luxury."

Breakfast is provided, and the tables fill up fast around 7:00 A.M. Beans, pork, and pancakes are served on tin plates, and an odd concoction some call "pea tea" is passed off as coffee. No salt, ketchup, or any condiments are provided. There are no women in this establishment, and the cooking, serving, and cleaning (such as it is) is performed by men. Sonora also has about ten gambling dens offering roulette, monte, faro, poker, and so on.

*Traveler's warning:* Crime is rampant in many of these gold country towns since most do not have police, sheriffs, or a military presence to keep desperados in line. Crime statistics illustrate this point. During only one week in July 1850, two miners from Massachusetts had their throats slit in Sonora, and a man from Chile was shot to death in a gunfight over a game of cards. In addition, a French miner stabbed a Mexican man over a mining claim. Meanwhile in Marysville, an astounding seventeen murders were committed in seven days.

## Memories for a Lifetime

From Marysville to Sonora, tourists will find a variety of hotels, restaurants, and saloons, many struggling to accommodate visitors under difficult circumstances in isolated wilderness areas. While beds may be uncomfortable—and prices high—California gold country offers tourists some of the finest scenery in the world. Whether you are coming to the area to make a fortune digging gold or simply for the enrichment of travel, visitors to California gold country will experience sights and sounds that will provide memories for a lifetime.

# CHAPTER EIGHT

# Mining Gold

Since most visitors to gold country are here to find riches, a discussion of mining methods will help potential prospectors. As every successful miner knows, finding gold requires dedication, hard work, and—most importantly—luck. The gold region encompasses thousands of square miles, and although it is common to hear rumors about miners finding twenty-pound nuggets or making $5,000 a day, the reality is that most are lucky to make a few dollars a day, laboring endless hours in harsh conditions. But with gold trading in San Francisco at about $16 an ounce, there is no shortage of men—and a few women—willing to try their hand at mining.

## Panning for Gold

A variety of techniques are used to separate gold from gravel depending on the location and surrounding terrain. The easiest gold to find is located in riverbeds and is referred to as placer gold. For removing these tiny flakes of wealth, panning is the tried-and-true method. Gold panners simply need to purchase a shovel, a pick, a knife, a pry bar, and a heavy metal pan, although some miners have found success panning with Indian baskets, tin cups, old hats, and even blankets.

Panning is based on the fact that gold is heavier than the surrounding gravel. Gold is carried by river water, but often its weight causes it to sink into deep cracks in the river bottom or wedges between tree roots, downed logs, or other obstacles. It may also be found in dirt near rivers, in ancient dry riverbeds, or in canyons and washes that flow only when it rains.

To pan for placer gold, miners dig up a quantity of what they hope is gold-bearing sand, gravel, and mud. Dumping the mixture into the gold pan, held at a 45-degree angle, the miner adds a steady stream of water from the river to wash

*Gold miners pan for gold at a river dig.*

out the lighter dirt. The heavy gold sinks to the bottom edge of the tilted pan. After all the sediment is removed, lucky miners will find gleaming flakes of gold and, possibly, a nugget.

Panning requires patience, skill, and much physical labor. Most miners sift through an average of about fifty pans worth of dirt during every ten-hour day. To perform the work, you should expect to be out in the withering sun and to stoop or squat in icy river water for hours on end, constantly shaking or rotating the pan.

Panners often shovel more than two thousand pounds of sand, silt, and gravel every day just to find enough gold to pay

for the expensive food found in most mining towns. Some miners pan week after week and find nothing at all. A few lucky forty-niners strike it rich in a very short time, inspiring others to continue at this difficult task.

*Mining tip:* Keep your gold pan clean. Any oil or grease (even from dirty hands) in the pan will attract gold flakes. Since oil floats, these flakes will be washed out of the pan immediately.

## Staking Your Claim

Early on, miners realized that reddish-brown dirt is more likely to contain gold. They are also able to distinguish gold from fool's gold (iron pyrite) by the fact that gold is soft and malleable and will flatten when struck with a hammer. Pyrite, on the other hand, simply shatters.

When miners do find "pay dirt" in a particular place, they stake a claim by driving stakes into the ground or laying personal property on the area to mark their spot. The next step is to register the spot with the mining camp's claims office. While claims may be as large as fifty square feet, great riches have been found in gold-bearing holes of only ten feet.

Miners are allowed only one claim, and if the forty-niner does not return to this site for one week, he may lose it, unless he is sick. (Oftentimes, if there is a dispute over who owns a claim, another miner or group of miners will help settle the argument.) The greatest problem for newcomers is finding any unclaimed land at all, let alone land in a promising area.

## The Rocker and the Long Tom

Although panning is simple and requires little investment, most of the gold that may be found this way has long since been removed by the swarms of miners that have invaded gold country since 1849. A better method for sifting through tons of sand, gravel, and mud requires a wooden rocker or cradle, so called because it resembles a baby's crib mounted on rockers. Rockers, rectangular boxes about three feet long, allow miners to sift through much greater quantities of gold—up to two hundred bucketfuls a day.

Cradles require two to four workers to operate efficiently. Two miners dig up gold-bearing dirt while a third shovels it into a bucket and pours it into a tray called a hopper that has small holes punched in its flat tin bottom. The third worker then scoops up several buckets full of water and pours them over the hopper. A fourth worker quickly rocks the device back and forth with a handle. This causes the smaller chunks of mixture to fall onto the angled apron, which resembles a picture

*Miners can wash more gold away than they find through the inefficient method of panning.*

## Minding the Mining Laws

*Visitors to gold country who wish to do some prospecting would be well advised to learn the basic laws that govern mining claims. The following laws were passed by the miners of Springfield and reprinted in* The Forty-Niners *by William Weber Johnson.*

A claim for mining purposes within this district shall not exceed one hundred square feet to each man. . . .

No man within the bounds of this district shall hold more than one claim. . . .

Each and every man holding a claim within the bounds of this district shall work one day out of every three, or employ a substitute; otherwise such claims shall be forfeited. . . .

Each and every man holding a claim within the bounds of this district, shall designate such claims by erecting good and substantial stakes at each corner of their claims, or dig a ditch around said claim. . . .

When any dispute arises concerning claims, and either party shall refuse to refer such dispute to a committee of five, two to be chosen by each party and the fifth to be chosen by the other four, the party so refusing shall forfeit all right to such claim in dispute. . . .

A standing committee of ten [shall] be appointed, to whom complaints shall be made in all mining disputes, and it shall be their especial duty to see [the above article] enforced, and that said committee [shall] be empowered to summon a posse at any time when necessary to assist them in the discharge of their duty. . . .

[It is] Resolved, That [these laws] be published in the Sonora Herald, and that 500 copies be printed in handbills.

frame covered with canvas. Tiny bits of gold dust are trapped in the canvas while the larger chunks wash onto a sluice, a long, angled tray set with a series of wooden rods called riffle bars. Lighter particles flow over the riffles, while the chunks of gold are trapped behind them. Several times a day, the work stops while the rocker is emptied of its riches.

Rockers cost about $2 to build but may sell for up to $100 in gold country, where the materials are scarce. Travelers would be wise to find plans for such devices, pick up the raw materials in San Francisco or Sacramento, and then ship wood, tin, and canvas to the goldfields for assembly. As with many other endeavors, some men have made more money building and shipping rockers than those who work them sixty hours a week.

Rockers perform well where water is scarce. But where rivers flow aplenty, miners enlist a device known as the Long Tom. These simple gold extractors, about fifteen feet long, twenty inches wide, and six inches deep, work like rockers. Instead of

*Mountaineers use the cradle rocking technique to search for gold.*

requiring workers to pour water over the dirt, however, rivers are diverted into narrow channels to flow over the Long Tom, which is laid in the small water-way. And instead of rocking the Long Tom, several miners simply agitate the dirt, mud, and gravel with their shovels. The material then passes over a small metal plate with half-inch holes, called a riddle, which separates out the smaller particles. Finally, the dirt is washed onto a five-foot sluice with riffle bars, where the gold is trapped. Several times a day,

this material is shoveled out and refined in a regular rocker.

## Separating Gold from Quartz

In some areas of gold country, every square inch of stream and shore has been claimed, so prospective miners will have to use more extravagant methods for finding their fortunes.

Gold that is trapped in hard rock quartz is more difficult to remove and requires investment in a machine called an *arrastra*. This device, first perfected by

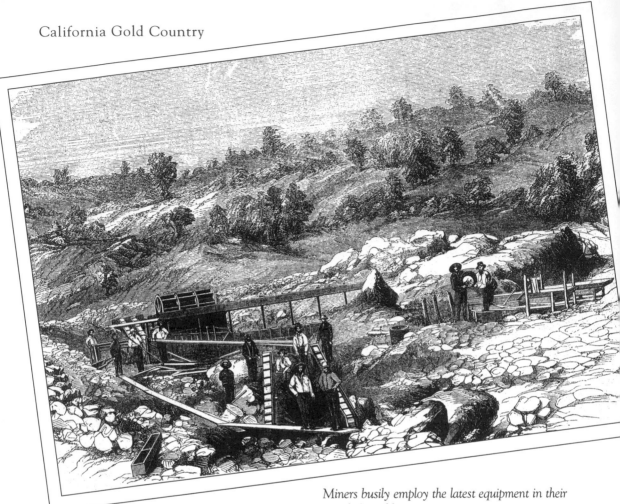

*Miners busily employ the latest equipment in their search for gold.*

Mexican miners, is like a gristmill. Instead of grain, however, finger-sized chunks of gold-bearing quartz are laid between the stones. The top stone is harnessed by way of a long pole to a mule or other animal that constantly walks around in a circle, pulverizing the quartz and gold into a fine dust.

Skilled craftsmen from Chile have introduced an improved version of the *arrastra* that uses a carved stone wheel that may be from five to ten feet in diameter. Instead of using flat stones atop one

another, the Chilean wheel rolls like a wagon wheel over a round iron floor, pivoting around a central spindle. The "Chile mill" can crush five tons of quartz in a single day but requires high-grade ore to be profitable.

Grinding wheels produce dust that must then be washed in rockers to separate the gold. Another way to separate the mineral wealth is to combine the rock dust with mercury. Gold adheres to the mercury while the quartz dust will not. The final gold may then be separated from the mercury by squeezing through a cheesecloth bag.

A more efficient method of separating the gold from the mercury involves a heat device called a retort. This device is fed with ball-sized globs of amalgam that are heated to molten temperatures in a special furnace. Since mercury liquefies at a much lower temperature, it vaporizes into the air, leaving a porous chunk of gold behind. The mercury gas flows through a cooling chamber, much like a liquor still, and is collected in a bucket for reuse.

*Warning:* Mercury is a highly toxic substance that can cause brain damage, liver damage, insanity, and even death if breathed, absorbed through the skin, or otherwise ingested. Mining towns are rife with miners who are "off their rockers" because of mercury poisoning.

## Into the Earth

At this time, surface mining is yielding constantly diminishing returns. Areas that were swarming with miners and

## Failure at the Dams

*In his book* Pen-Knife Sketches or Chips Off the Old Block, *Alonzo "Old Block" Delano describes an enterprising group who dammed a river hoping to find gold and were rewarded with nothing after months of labor.*

New diggings have been discovered, and a plan is in embryo to *dam the river*. And why was it not thought of before? Turn the stream and get gold by bushels! The originator is a genius; he is looked upon as such, and a company of sly ones is soon got up, and the work commenced. This requires weeks and months of severe labor, and an outlay of money—all that has been made before by patient toil, and perhaps more. But the operation is sure; there is no mistake, and at it we go. Twenty thousand dollars is spent, the labor is done, the water is finally turned, and with much hope, though with a few misgivings, a hole is sunk in the very bed of the stream. Every eye is strained to get a glimpse of the scales; many pans full are tried, and gracious Heavens! there is not a dime to be found! Shaft after shaft is sunk, but "Dame Fortune's golden smile" is not there, and the sad reality comes in the shape of [bills due], from the traders, for flour, pork and pickles, kindly furnished our mess, with the full hope of securing an honest profit to themselves. Dead broke; not a dime to pay a debt, and the company dissolve and disperse, after months of labor, disheartened and in debt, bestowing a hearty and audible d—n on all dams.

machines only last year are now as deserted as Death Valley in August. Instead, individual miners are starting to see large companies from New York and London investing up to $200,000 to dig deep gold mines in the area. These companies may hire up to one hundred miners, and some of those who have had no luck panning, rocking, and milling are finding work with these large companies that are digging, blasting, and tunneling into the earth.

# Notes

**Chapter One: A Brief History
of California Gold Country**
1. Quoted in Malcolm J. Rohrbough,
   *Days of Gold*. Berkeley: University
   of California Press, 1997, p. 24.

**Chapter Three: The Overland
Route to Gold Country**
2. William G. Johnston, *Overland to
   California*. Oakland, CA: Biobooks,
   1948, p. 154.

**Chapter Four: The Sea
Route to Gold Country**
3. Fayette Robinson and Franklin Street,
   *The Gold Mines of California: Two
   Guidebooks*. New York: Promontory
   Press, 1974, p. 102.
4. Robinson and Street, *The Gold Mines
   of California*, p. 102.
5. Quoted in Salvador A. Ramirez, ed.,
   *From New York to San Francisco via
   Cape Horn in 1849*. Carlsbad, CA:
   Tentacled Press, 1985, p. 17.
6. Franklin A. Buck, *A Yankee Trader
   in the Gold Rush*. Boston: Houghton
   Mifflin, 1930, p. 41.
7. Quoted in Ramirez, *From New York to
   San Francisco via Cape Horn in 1849*,
   p. 134.

**Chapter Five: Touring
San Francisco**
8. Hinton Helper, *Dreadful California*.
   Indianapolis: Bobbs-Merrill, 1948,
   p. 63.
9. Helper, *Dreadful California*, pp. 56–57.

**Chapter Six: Touring Sacramento**
10. Robinson and Street, *The Gold Mines
    of California*, p. 30.
11. Helper, *Dreadful California*, p. 112.
12. Quoted in Helper, *Dreadful California*,
    p. 108.
13. Quoted in Helper, *Dreadful California*,
    p. 108.
14. Quoted in Joann Levy, *They Saw
    the Elephant*. Hamden, CT: Archon
    Books, 1990, p. 138.
15. Quoted in Levy, *They Saw the Elephant*,
    p. 138.
16. Edwin Bryant, *What I Saw in California*.
    Palo Alto, CA: Lewis Osborne, 1967,
    p. 268.
17. Bryant, *What I Saw in California*,
    p. 271.

**Chapter Seven: Touring
Gold Country**
18. Helper, *Dreadful California*, pp. 118–19.

# For Further Reading

Connie Goldsmith, *Lost in Death Valley: The True Story of Four Families in California's Gold Rush*. Brookfield, CT: Twenty-First Century Books, 2001. The trials and tribulations of pioneers traveling through California's harsh desert on their way to gold country.

Tom Ito, *The California Gold Rush*. San Diego: Lucent Books, 1997. Events surrounding the nineteenth-century gold rush in California, the lifestyle of miners, and the phenomenon of boomtowns and ghost towns.

Liza Ketchum, *The Gold Rush*. Boston: Little, Brown, 1996. Based on the PBS television series *The West*, this book discusses events that drew tens of thousands of people to California and their effect on the Spanish settlers and the Native Americans who lived there.

Rosalyn Schanzer, ed., *Gold Fever*, Washington, DC: National Geographic Society, 1999. Illustrations and excerpts from letters, journals, and newspaper articles that relate the story of the gold rush.

Victoria Sherrow, *Life During the Gold Rush*. San Diego: Lucent Books, 1998. Describes the way people lived during the gold rush era, with eyewitness accounts, maps, and pictures.

Jerry Stanley, *Hurry Freedom: African Americans in Gold Rush California*. New York: Crown, 2000. Recounts the history of African Americans in California during the gold rush.

# Works Consulted

**Books**

Edwin Bryant, *What I Saw in California*. Palo Alto, CA: Lewis Osborne, 1967. Bryant walked the entire Oregon Trail and visited much of California while eloquently describing his experiences in this early eyewitness guide, originally published in 1848.

Franklin A. Buck, *A Yankee Trader in the Gold Rush*. Boston: Houghton Mifflin, 1930. A compilation of letters written by a successful trader as he traveled through San Francisco and gold country in the early 1850s.

Alonzo Delano, *Pen-Knife Sketches or Chips Off the Old Block*. San Francisco: Grabhorn Press, 1934. A series of humorous essays and illustrations concerning San Francisco and gold country. The author's widely published razor-sharp wit earned him fame and fortune, and he was a household name in California in the 1850s.

John Charles Frémont, *Report of the Exploring Expedition to the Rocky Mountains in the Year 1842, and to Oregon and North California in the Years 1843–44*. Washington, DC: Gales and Seaton, 1845. One of the first published books about the land and people west of the Rocky Mountains. This was a popular guide for the first forty-niners, who had little information about the trip that lay ahead.

Vincent E. Geiger and Wakeman Bryarly, *Trail to California*. New Haven: Yale University Press, 1945. The diary of two former soldiers as they made their way to California from the East Coast.

Hinton Helper, *Dreadful California*. Indianapolis: Bobbs-Merrill, 1948. An account of one traveler's negative experiences in California. The book's amusing subtitle explains the author's attitude: "Being a true and scandalous account of the barbarous civilization, licentious morals, crude manners and depravities, inclement climate and niggling resources, together with various other offensive and calamitous details of life in the Golden State."

William Weber Johnson, *The Forty-Niners*. Alexandria, VA: Time-Life Books, 1974. A colorful history of the California gold rush.

William G. Johnston. *Overland to California*. Oakland, CA: Biobooks, 1948. The diary of a man who crossed the Oregon Trail into California in 1849.

Joann Levy, *They Saw the Elephant*. Hamden, CT: Archon Books, 1990. The story of women during the California gold rush, with hundreds of eyewitness observations taken mostly from letters and correspondence.

Mary Rockwood Powers, *A Woman's Overland Journal to California*. Fairfield, WA: Ye Galleon Press, 1985. A diary of a cross-country trip with vivid descriptions of the beauty and hardships the author experienced along the way.

Salvador A. Ramirez, ed., *From New York to San Francisco via Cape Horn in 1849*. Carlsbad, CA: Tentacled Press, 1985. The eyewitness accounts of four men who sailed to California at the beginning of the gold rush.

Fayette Robinson and Franklin Street, *The Gold Mines of California: Two Guidebooks*. New York: Promontory Press, 1974. A reprint of two original travel guides to the gold country: *California and Its Gold Regions* (1849) and *California in 1850 Compared to What It Was in 1849, with a Glimpse at Its Future Destiny* (1850).

Malcolm J. Rohrbough, *Days of Gold*. Berkeley: University of California Press, 1997. A well-researched history of the California gold rush.

Dudley T. Ross, *The Golden Gazette*. Fresno: Valley, 1978. Genuine articles from various gold country newspapers published between 1848 and 1857, with hundreds of events concerning mining, boomtowns, crime, social events, immigrants and more.

Joseph E. Ware, *The Emigrants' Guide to California*. New York: Da Capo Press, 1972. One of the original travel guides specifically written for forty-niners on their way to California's gold country.

**Internet Sources**

Oregon-California Trail Association, "Forty Mile Desert." http://calcite. rocky.edu. An excellent virtual tour of the long Oregon and California

Trails. Clicking on a given spot provides links with pictures and eye-witness descriptions of various landmarks.

John Sinclair, "Log Entries for December, 1846." http://members. aol.com/DanMRosen. Diary entries of a member of the Donner party with chilling details of frostbite, starvation, and cannibalism.

# Index

# Picture Credits

# About the Author

Stuart A. Kallen is the author of more than 150 nonfiction books for children and young adults. He has written on topics ranging from the theory of relativity to rock-and-roll history, to life on the American frontier. In addition, Mr. Kallen has written award-winning children's videos and television scripts. In his spare time, Mr. Kallen is a singer/songwriter/guitarist in San Diego, California.